"Be open to challenge, to critic  of new evidence or compelling whether or not they persuade y and respect them despite your disagreements. Cornel West and I, in our work together, have proclaimed these principles. Now Ulrich Lehner has provided a manual—a how-to guide—for implementing them in one's life. It's a book that intellectually and morally serious people of all ages will want to read."

—**Robert P. George**, Princeton University

"Against the deranged and destructive expressions of post-truth and brazen public lying in recent years, Lehner insists that we all can and must improve our thinking and accountability to truth—and in this highly accessible text he tells us how. The issues addressed here are of utmost importance. Individual people, churches, society, and the world will be much better off if this book has the impact that it deserves."

—**Christian Smith**, University of Notre Dame

"This is a fresh and wondrous introduction to philosophical thinking, a true delight, a cool and restorative oasis in what's too often a vast desert of dry pedantic texts. Lehner shares his own enthusiasm for rational thought in a manner that's both endearing and contagious. Philosophy is a way of living in the world that requires both humility and confidence, wonder and reason. This book beautifully shows us that path and can help us all walk it better. It will have a powerful, positive effect in our precise cultural moment and long into the future."

—**Tom Morris**, author of *Plato's Lemonade Stand* and *The Oasis Within*

"Our nation suffers from a rationality deficit. We feel, we don't think. Emotivism rules the day. Lehner has produced a beautiful response. *Think Better* explains why reasoning is so important, and how we all can exercise our rational capabilities better. A mix of history, philosophy, practical advice, and personal experience, this book is perfect for the introductory college classroom and the lay reader looking to, well, think better. Warmly recommended."

—**Ryan T. Anderson**, president, Ethics and Public Policy Center

THINK
BETTER

UNLOCKING
THE POWER OF
REASON

ULRICH L. LEHNER

Baker Academic
a division of Baker Publishing Group
Grand Rapids, Michigan

© 2021 by Ulrich L. Lehner

Published by Baker Academic
a division of Baker Publishing Group
PO Box 6287, Grand Rapids, MI 49516-6287
www.bakeracademic.com

Printed in the United States of America

Library of Congress Cataloging-in-Publication Data
Names: Lehner, Ulrich L., 1976– author.
Title: Think better : unlocking the power of reason / Ulrich L. Lehner.
Description: Grand Rapids, Michigan : Baker Academic, a division of Baker Publishing Group, [2021] | Includes bibliographical references and index.
Identifiers: LCCN 2021017456 | ISBN 9781540964762 (paperback) | ISBN 9781540964779 (casebound) | ISBN 9781493433452 (ebook)
Subjects: LCSH: Thought and thinking. | Reasoning. | Knowledge, Theory of.
Classification: LCC B105.T54 L44 2021 | DDC 153.4/2—dc23
LC record available at https://lccn.loc.gov/2021017456

Baker Publishing Group publications use paper produced from sustainable forestry practices and post-consumer waste whenever possible.

21   22   23   24   25   26   27   7   6   5   4   3   2   1

Contents

Introduction

EMPOWERING MINDS

As you think, so shall you become." The first time I read this quote that some attribute to Bruce Lee, I was struck by how profound it was. It captures the wisdom of ancient Eastern and Western philosophy alike that our life "is what our thoughts make it" (Marcus Aurelius, 121–80 CE).[1] The way to more powerful and productive reasoning lies in using it to its fullest potential. For that purpose, we have to find out what reasoning is, how it works, and in what instances we can use it. By doing so, we will not only identify strategies to empower our minds but also begin to walk the path of philosophy and begin the search for wisdom. This quest is far from impractical because it enables us to become more focused in our work, find peace in our minds, and explore the hidden creativity of our souls. And believe me, I am speaking as someone who has found such empowerment.

For almost all my adult life I have engaged with questions of knowledge and truth, philosophy here, philosophy there, but only last year did the power of reasoning really become clear to me. I sat in the chair of a psychologist's office. He was evaluating a long list of tests I had taken for the last four hours. My eyes were fixed on him when he finally looked up, smiled, and said, "Your intuition was right. You definitely have ADHD!" I was not surprised, and neither was my family, who had always suspected it. Nevertheless, what amazed me was how bad I was at doing commonplace things, such as paying attention and being able to listen to others. Yet how had I been able to become a renowned researcher with these deficits? My psychologist told me the answer: "Because you must have developed behaviors that compensate for your lack of attention. And these behaviors made you successful."

This revelation made me reflect on my life and how I had reached the point I was at now. What allowed me to function in the world I was in? How was I able to hold a position at one of America's greatest universities? After a short time, I realized how I was able to cope. Since my earliest school days, I looked for behaviors that helped me control my ADHD impulses, without even knowing it. Suddenly it made sense why I found the rigorous routine of my old grandfather—including him wearing a tie every day until he was in his nineties—so impressive and worthy of imitation. I realized how I learned in church that rituals can structure your life and discipline your mind, and so on. Yet what seems to have been the most crucial influence was having been exposed to good reasoning, first at home and then at school. At my German high school, we read Plato and Aristotle in the original Greek in tenth grade! Ever since my teachers first gave me *The Apology of Socrates* by Plato, I was captivated by the power of reasoning and wanted to learn as much about it as I could. I was hooked!

Philosophical reasoning empowered me to develop discipline not only in thinking but also in observing: I knew I could pay attention to details that fascinated me—as every person with ADHD can testify to—but philosophy allowed me to do it with a method. Don't get me wrong—I had to work at least twice as hard as any other student to understand things I found boring, but I did it. Wrapping my head around geometry in high school was so stressful for me that even years later I had nightmares about it. Nevertheless, the tools of philosophy helped me to stay somewhat on course and not drift away completely every time something interesting popped into my head; they empowered me to navigate these difficult waters. I am convinced that the structure they provided me with was the key to my success in high school and beyond. I sometimes tell my doctoral students, "There were smarter students than me in the doctoral classes I took, yet they all lacked perseverance and structure. This is the real key to success." Philosophical reasoning helped me to organize my mind, my studies, and my research. It empowered me to have a career that others were unable to achieve.

I am living proof that ordering one's thought leads to happiness. Reasoning not only helped me with my studies but also improved the quality of my life. Reasoning leads to joy. The joy of mastering something always reminds me of diving. Plunging into the ocean equipped with a wet suit, goggles, and an oxygen tank opens up a new world of hidden colors, fish, corals, and rocks. Philosophical thinking is very similar—it invites you to dive deep into the structure of things. Just like with diving, however, you need to have the proper equipment, some principles, and a map. In this book, I hope to show you that reason allows you to discover answers to questions such as, Who am I? What can I know? What is good? What can I hope for?

Diving below is only one aspect of reasoning. The other is gaining perspective from above. I associate this with hiking in the mountains, probably because I grew up near the Alps. Not much compares to the feeling of accomplishment and awe when you have made it to the top. Adrenaline rushes through your body after the exhausting climb, your muscles ache, but once you see the landscape below, you lose yourself in the beauty in front of you. You see the different shades of snow around you, the vegetation along the mountainside, and far away the crystal waters of a lake. Only the jackdaws soaring in the thin air above you have a better view, seeing how even the mountaintop is connected to the landscape, seeing things as a whole. Philosophy tries to accomplish this as well, not just diving into the structure of the world but also putting it all in perspective, understanding how things hang together. It is the ultimate way of holistic thinking.

Perhaps you are still not sure whether you want to continue with this book because it sounds too "brainy." After all, what exactly do philosophers look for, and why would it be helpful for me to adopt some of their tools? Shouldn't we instead imitate the hard sciences, which boast of their discoveries? But have you asked yourself what is at the beginning of a scientist's work? You can't just wake up one morning and decide to find a cure for cancer; you have to have a plan. You have to begin by making an observation, asking a question, forming a hypothesis, testing it, and so forth. What is it that makes the scientist ask the question in the first place? Humans desire to know not just facts, but the *whatness* of things, their inner reasons and causes. We want to know what this or that type of cancer is, how it develops and why, or why and how a plant produces this or that enzyme if it could also survive without it. This drive to know the *whatness* of the world moves us to dive into the structure of the world and examine the characteristics of something. And thus, the scientist also begins with *philosophical* questions and assumptions: By arranging a lab experiment, I have already made the philosophical assumption that I can trust my senses, that I am able to correctly assess the world outside my brain and thus can read the lab instruments properly. Moreover, I base my whole experiment on the assumption that the aspect of the world I have in my lab is intelligible and discoverable. Once we begin to see that every search for knowledge is based on certain underlying assumptions, we can start to examine and question what our other assumptions are—for example, what we believe politically—and thus are better able to understand those who disagree with us. Only if I gain insight into my own beliefs will I be able to also look rationally at another person's perspective. I will also discover which of my beliefs are irrational, which ones weigh me down and keep me from becoming the person I want to be. This will help me to express my thoughts in an orderly fashion so that I will be understood by others. Reason helps us to become better human beings and achieve a better quality of life.

The great philosophers have realized that every one of us has a desire to question things. We never stop asking questions. And it all begins with a sense of awe: we are intrigued by something we don't know but desire to know better. That's what drove the great physicists to discover the nature of matter, Watson and Crick to shed light on what DNA is, and Wernher von Braun to help build the first rockets that transported humans to the moon.[2] Discoveries begin with curiosity and awe about the mysteries we encounter and about which we want to know more. Nevertheless, the questions a philosopher asks are different from those a scientist would ask. While the biologist studies living things, the philosopher desires to know *what* things are, and *what* life is; philosophers use their mind, not a lab. The sciences, just like the humanities, look at very specific objects, while philosophy looks at the bedrock of things and the foundation of it all, and at how these things hang together in the whole of reality.

Lastly, I think that good reasoning would help this country. Millions of Americans seem to no longer want to listen to each other or even contemplate any counterargument to their ideas about life, liberty, and politics. We are stuck in a deadlock of partisan polarization in which we focus only on information that confirms our biases instead of critically engaging with what challenges them. Unlocking the powers of reason offers a way out of such a standstill because it empowers people to scrutinize texts (and images), distinguish aspects of questions, identify hidden presuppositions, and reject fallacious conclusions. A world dominated by half-truths and fake news cries out for more reason! About three-quarters of Americans label people from the other political party as "closed-minded," but at the same time, they detest the polarization of their country.[3] They clearly see polarization as a problem but do not know how to overcome it.[4] I suggest that more and better reasoning might be a way forward: adopting more rationality not only aids the common good but can also lead to *mutual* learning, tolerance, and empathy as well as undermine prejudices and false assumptions. Reason has the power to bring people together and create unity because it is a gift we all share.

Since this book came about as a result of some soul searching, I wanted it to be personal and not driven by philosophical jargon or academic expectations. That's why I laid out what I consider helpful for myself, my kids, and my students in short chapters but in a way that lets the reader *join* the quest and take possession of the discoveries for herself.

It's needless to say that you might not agree with all my conclusions. But if this book helps you see that the diversity of our minds makes this world beautiful and that reasoning is a powerful tool for the good, then it has fulfilled its purpose.

Knowledge Is the Basis of Good Reasoning

Reasoning is not done in a vacuum. It always requires knowledge. I can only pursue certain ideas or plans if I know something about them first and then have the desire to inquire further. Therefore, if we really want to think more clearly, it is crucial to understand what knowledge is. Otherwise, we might search for knowledge either in the wrong places or with the wrong strategies.

Compare the powerful tool of reason with a knife: With a dull knife, you cannot even cut a simple roll. You might be able to use it for spreading some butter, but that is about it. Reason *without* knowledge is very much like a dull knife: it can't cut through the layers of information to get to the truth of the matter. By figuring out how knowledge works, we learn how to sharpen the knife of reason and how to use it properly.

Everyone already has some vague understanding of what it means to know something. Knowing is always intending something; it is intentional. For example, when I say, "I know how to repair cars," the repair skills are the object of my knowledge. (More about such intentionality in chap. 5.) Moreover, knowing implies a profound familiarity with an object: "If you can name the cause of something, you have understood it," as Aristotle once said.[1] Applied to the car, this principle means the person who knows automotive repairs understands *how* the whole machine works. She is able to accurately pinpoint various malfunctions and their causes, and of course she knows how to resolve the issues. Therefore, a student who merely regurgitates information does not "know," because he lacks deeper understanding of the object.

Knowledge Is Conversational

How does such understanding come about? The answer to this riddle lies in the fact that *all* our understanding is expressed in words. Words are signs used and created by humans to find orientation in the world or to communicate with each other. Consequently, we have to take a close look at how humans use language to communicate with each other, because without such interactions there would be no knowledge.

For any statement or judgment about the world or ourselves, about real or abstract things, we use words. Whether it is a tree, my experience of tooth pain, the law of gravity, or a mathematical law, without words we would not know the world. You can do a simple experiment yourself: Stare outside your window. You will have a sensory impression, but the moment you focus on something, you use words (e.g., when you are looking at the car driving by, even if you just think "car"). There is consequently no knowledge without language. Most importantly, however, we use language when we communicate with another person, in a *conversation*. Without language, we could not communicate complex messages to each other.[2] Humans learn from each other, and because we are social animals, the mystery of how knowledge works can be found in our conversations.

We all have conversations, but what is a conversation exactly? How would you describe the nature of a conversation to someone? A good starting point would be to describe it as an exchange of words between at least two people who are also listeners. In order to comprehend the content of the conversation, it is not enough that I am able to listen (my bird can listen too). I also have to be able to understand what is being said (the meaning of the words). I must be able to understand whether my counterpart describes something, shares with me an evaluation, expresses his feelings, and so forth. A parrot might repeat a sentence, but a human has the ability to bring what she has heard "into" her own self: she is able to react to the sentences by pondering their meaning and reflecting on them. Thus a conversation necessarily presupposes at least two persons who are independent beings. When I say, "You have made an excellent point," I recognize that I am speaking to a being who is independent of me, endowed with the same basic knowledge of language as I am. As August Brunner said, "The other, the Thou is therefore a center just like me, a center which owns itself and has power over its acts. . . . The Thou presents to us a reality which in no way is a mere projection or the creation of my fantasy."[3]

Having the ability to open oneself up to other such independent beings, or *Thous*, and to the world is a crucial element of being human. Without it, there would be no conversation and, consequently, no knowledge, and especially no rich personal life. Even if we withdraw into the silence of the mountains and carry our thoughts with us, "we always take our language along, without which we cannot think" and which cannot work without openness to other things. With such openness also comes the realization that I am a self and that through an encounter with other I's, I can learn or get to know more about myself and the world we share.[4]

Conversations happen . . . in time. It might seem unnecessary to state this obvious fact, but it is an important characteristic. Talking with somebody happens in the flow of time, where one word follows the next, with a pause, a question being answered, an argument rebuffed, and so forth. The meaning of what we say is not so much tied up in individual words but in the whole string of words we produce. "Only at the end of a sentence, when the sound of the words has already died away and exists no more, do the words gain meaning."[5] In order to understand sentences and interactions, however, we obviously need the ability to remember what was said before and keep the conversation and its meaning present to our mind so that we can also anticipate to a certain extent how it will continue. Memory is the ability to *own our past* and *recognize it as such*. Memory is tremendously powerful and is essential to our quality of life, which makes illnesses such as dementia all the more tragic.[6] Something in the flow of a conversation remains stable, and that is the self. Only from such an unchanging perspective am I able to judge change, use my memory, and anticipate events: only because I am an independent self do I understand that the person I am speaking with is going to propose a business deal to me. I can anticipate it because I remember his behavior on other occasions, and in those he always suggested a business deal. Conversations therefore require *selfs*, which means that despite all advances in technology, we will never be able to have a real conversation with a computer.

How to Train Your Will, or When It Is Better to Shut Up

A conversation happens between at least two people who usually alternate between speaking and listening. If I constantly shut down the dialogue with my own monologue, however, I lose the chance of learning anything new and run the risk of getting stuck in false assumptions. A crucial component for acquiring more accurate and complete knowledge, therefore, is the ability to listen, which requires humility.

In the last few decades, a number of philosophers have highlighted the close connection between such virtues as listening/humility and knowledge (*virtue epistemology*). In antiquity, the method for reshaping one's behavior was called *askēsis*, and it was a mindset for training the virtuous self. In the fourth century BCE, Aristotle argued that virtue was not about the quality of an action but rather about the quality of a person. Virtues, such as justice, prudence, fortitude, and so forth, could shape and transform a person, a bit like how regular exercise changes an athlete's whole body. A way of intensifying and speeding up growth in virtue was deliberate training by *askēsis*. It entailed giving up certain goods for a defined period of time, such as eating meat. By doing so, one not only became more appreciative of the good one had given up—in this case the ability to enjoy a steak—but first and foremost one trained the *will*. It is, after all, our will that *makes us do things*. Even if I do not want to silence my dialogue partner, I still might not have the willpower and virtue to hold my tongue and listen. The philosopher Immanuel Kant calls this practice the "cultivation" of virtue.[7]

Asceticism as a training of the will makes us more aware of our own self *and* of our actions. It gives us a magnifying glass to see what was hitherto covered up in the rubbish pile of our psyche. By identifying *ascetic* goals, I acquire mental discipline and become profoundly aware of what I am capable of, both the good and the bad. I could, for example, abstain from gossiping about others. This might help me realize that my gossip was just a way of expressing my own unhappiness and jealousy . . . and so forth. Such ascetical exercises train our mind for disciplined thinking, too, because they make us cautious, curtail overconfidence, and improve our ability to listen and be more empathetic.[8]

If this doesn't convince you, perhaps you can think about asceticism from the perspective of *external influences*: social media, the workplace, and other external influences constantly throw images and texts at us; our everyday experience forces us to tune many of them out in order to focus on our job and our family duties. If we, however, become *complacent* enough to no longer actively tune out such influences, they will overpower us. As long as you are aware of your filter, you can adjust it (e.g., by ascetic practices), but once you've lost it, you can easily become sucked into a hole of misery. Instead of tuning out things like social media influences, we become enslaved to them and to the material world. We become blind to values such as beauty and truth because we are too focused on what we should buy or invest our money in. Then we can no longer appreciate the beauty of snow falling or the wonder of a spiderweb on our window, or, even worse, we become deaf to the needs of a spouse who would like our attention.[9]

The better we prepare our mind to properly receive the impulses from the world outside, the more "realistic" we are, and the more appropriately we are able to act in conversation. By bracketing my self-interest for the moment and letting something "speak" to me, I not only practice a form of asceticism, but I also learn to appreciate things on their own terms. One easy way of demonstrating this is to ask yourself whether you can experience the beauty even of a gray and dark day in the city, or of a rock pigeon. Can you still perceive their beauty, or do you view almost everything under the perspective of how *you* can use it or how it serves *your* purposes? If you feel that the scales are in favor of what some call "me-ism," then you might be attached to material goods in a way that subdues not only your ethics but also your mind! Instead of "breathing with" the things and people we encounter—that's the original meaning of *con-spire*—you simply breathe *at* them because you only know how to use them. Instead of cooperating with the world, you are trying to conquer it; the worst, however, is that because of these shackles you have lost the liberty to encounter a world in which truth, beauty, and goodness still matter.[10]

We started this chapter by searching for how knowledge works, and we found that it is always expressed in language. Language, however, exists in and for conversation, and there is no knowledge without conversation, because without conversation there would be no language. Now we can turn to knowledge itself and ask what it really is.

2

Have Realistic Goals and Humility

"All I know is that I know nothing." Socrates made this statement in the fourth century BCE to show that our knowledge is fragmentary.[1] The more I find out about my body and my genetic history, the more I do not know; the more a geologist finds out about the tectonic plates on earth, the more questions arise. There is no end to knowledge! This acknowledgment, however, should not make us despair. Rather it should entice us to identify what we want to know and what we can know, and thus help us set realistic goals. Only if we have a clear goal will we be able to pursue it, and only if we are capable of pursuing that goal will we not fall into despair and frustration. Thus what Socrates said is not something that hinders me in my search for knowledge, but rather is a very *practical program* for empowering my mind. It teaches me to be realistic about what to expect and to remain humble about my own shortcomings, and it reminds me that whatever I discover is only a fragment of the whole.

Knowing Always Desires Truth

In order to develop our minds, we need to give our minds realistic goals. These goals are the objects on which we focus. This focus is called *intentionality*, which is a crucial concept in philosophy. Do we find intentionality in other human actions, and if so, is it the same kind of intentionality? The first comparison that comes to my mind concerns our emotions. When I feel an emotion such as joy, I am *affected* by a sentiment or mood. Something moves me from within whether I intend it to or not—and this is the opposite of intentionality. It is only after I am affected by a feeling that I can direct it toward an object. For example, I feel angry about something that is taking place in my town, and then I can direct it toward a responsible solution as its object. Also, feelings remain inside us; they cannot be shared with another person in the same way knowledge can. You might object and say, "Of course I can talk about my feelings," and you would be right, but when you do, you share a statement *about* your feelings, not the feeling *itself*. Feelings remain within *me*—and *me* alone—always.

Knowing is also different from wanting. When I want to buy a new book, I have an object in mind and I aim at something, which is definitely intentional, but just like with feelings, this intentionality remains *internal*. Although I can speak *about* my wants, I cannot share the *experience of wanting*. Moreover, wanting always intends action, like me buying a new book, which is not necessarily the case with knowledge. Finally, I can even desire and want things that are not possible, such as being invisible, because wanting is all about possession of something but it doesn't have to be real. No one, however, searches for knowledge about something they know is false or imaginary. And thus we arrive at our first definition: *Knowledge aims at knowing something true about an object.*

Truth is also what differentiates knowing from mere thinking: although I am using my brain to gain knowledge, *thinking alone* is not necessarily aiming at truth. For example, I can think about humanoid silicon-based aliens independently from whether or not such life forms can even exist. Yet when we get to know something, we *acquire* some truth. You might interject now and ask, "What is truth?"—and rightly so, because we haven't explained it yet. There are libraries full of books about truth theories, and different philosophers will give you different answers. I believe that if we say a statement is true, we mean that it corresponds with the reality it describes: *Ulrich's head is nearly bald* is only true if there is not much hair left on Ulrich's head. If you ask my kids, they will tell you, "It's so true!" This should suffice in this book as a working definition of truth.[2]

When I talk with somebody, I am not just reciting a poem or the lyrics of a song; I am forming sentences that are meant to be understood. Whenever these sentences make a claim about things in the world, about things in my mind (a dream), or about something abstract (like a geometrical figure), I am formulating a *truth claim*. My sentence is true if it adequately describes my object—otherwise it is false. If I ask my friend how to change the motor oil of my lawn mower, I am not asking for his abstract opinion but for his expert knowledge—his "know-how"! Certainly, we hold many opinions to be true, but if we are careful and honest, we will not mistake them for *secure* knowledge, for something that accurately corresponds to reality. We know intuitively that our opinions lack such accuracy.

Knowledge and Incompetence

All languages express our searching for knowledge and truth—we should stop and think about this for a moment. You only search for something you do *not* have; therefore, knowledge must be something we are *not* born with (or not much?) and thus have to acquire somehow. Truth has to be somehow plucked out of darkness; our mind *reveals* to us the truth it finds, and therefore we speak about the quest for truth and knowledge. Something that was hitherto unknown becomes known and thus somehow becomes part of ourselves. All too often, however, we act as if our mind were somehow immersed in the ocean of truth and we had all the answers.

At this point, we have become proud and no longer acknowledge that the search for knowledge is a never-ending quest. Much of what we know comes about after we have wrestled with ideas and discussed them passionately with others, but I have hardly ever found that important truths are discovered easily or without personal investment. The search for knowledge requires the will of an adventurer, of one willing to set sail in areas unknown, to take risks, and to broaden one's horizon. It makes it necessary to humble oneself and acknowledge that others might be right and we might be wrong.

Such an outlook on life is realistic because it takes the world around us seriously and is critical of what we might project on it. Without humility, it is easy to be overconfident and set un-realistic goals and expectations that are beyond our abilities to fulfill. Psychologists have even analyzed how much people mis-judge themselves. People who performed poorly on cognitive tests overestimated their performance by a factor of more than three. These findings suggest that many are unaware of their lack of competence and misjudge their intellectual faculties. When con-fronted with demanding tasks, they are consequently unable to fulfill them to the satisfaction of a supervisor or even themselves. The result is frustration and anger. Sound and sober reasoning, however, can help keep us grounded in reality because it demands that we at least occasionally question and assess our thoughts to see whether they accurately portray reality or whether we are constructing a fantasy world. Philosophy keeps us cognitively con-sistent, and Socrates's advice reminds us that if we are honest, we can identify "pockets of ignorance" in our lives as well as areas where we make incompetent decisions. This enables us to listen in conversation and to accept being corrected if needed.[3]

Nevertheless, knowledge also includes *confidence*, and that does not contradict what I said about humility. First of all, I have to have confidence that I can know and discover what is true. That is not an obvious statement, because the world does not have to be a place in which I can find truth; it does not have to be intelligible. So whenever I go on an adventure to search for knowledge, I also begin a journey *of trust and confidence in myself.* I must believe "I can find this out." This does not mean that we cannot use guidance and help—just like an adventurer takes a compass or a map along the way. Yet do we instill such confidence in our children and students? If we spoon-feed them "all they need to know," we rob them of the chance to find out things for themselves.

There is yet another dimension of confidence involved in knowledge. Once I have discovered something is true, I have a sense of confidence that is *not easily shaken.* The image that comes to my mind is that of taking possession of a pirate treasure, proudly sitting down on top of the chest. Rightly so, in one respect: you have searched and found. Good! But, if we remain sitting on the treasure chest, we might never know how much the treasure inside is really worth. Confidence in knowledge can make us easily proud and lead us to dismiss criticism. Certainly not every voice is equally worth listening to, but if we keep Socrates's warning in mind that all of our knowledge is fragmentary, then our confidence should at least never be unshakable. If we remain honest, there will always be a cloud of uncertainty hanging over it.

Nevertheless, we should also not too easily exchange our "treasure" for counterfeit. During philosophical discussions, I often encounter people who, instead of giving arguments, simply say, "Well, it could also be different." Let's say I have argued that whenever carbon-based conscious life (like that of us humans) exists, it comes with certain limitations such as pain, suffering, and death. You decide that you don't like my claim and counter my argument by saying, "Life does not have to be carbon based. It could be different." It certainly could, but I would have to take your criticism seriously only if you could show *how* other conscious life forms could exist and escape all limitations (silicon-based life perhaps?). Without giving arguments, the "It could be different!" is not a worthwhile interjection because it does not show me that you understand what constitutes life. For me to take you seriously would require that you give reasons for why you think such and such is possible. Most often the "It could be different" line is used to silence an opponent in a debate or to undermine her stance. Many people are not prepared to answer and thus fall silent and the silly and irrational "It could be different" line wins the day. Yet all you have to do to defend your stance is to force your opponent to name his reasons, and if he can't, you are entitled to dismiss his interjection as baseless.

Knowledge Is Not Piecemeal but Holistic

Considering all we have discussed so far, it becomes clear that we have varying degrees of confidence in our areas of knowledge; some things I am more confident about than others. If by *knowledge* I mean discovering a truth about something, then knowledge seems to be a way of gaining *insight* into things, which, as we saw in the previous chapter, comes about through the help of language and can be communicated to others without losing its content (like feelings or wants). Human knowledge is not restricted to material objects that we observe with our senses of sight, hearing, and so forth. In fact, knowledge derived from our senses can be easily manipulated or influenced. I remember distinctly how incapable I was of orienting myself in my own house after taking painkillers following a knee operation. Sensory impressions only become knowledge when we put them into language and integrate them into judgments, so that they are in principle communicable to others (e.g., "My office desk is brown"). Beyond the singular objects we stumble upon in this world, we can arrive at knowledge combining such experiences, which we call laws.

Laws, however, are immaterial, intellectual objects that I cannot touch, smell, or measure, and we will discuss them further in the next chapter. Much of our knowledge is immaterial/abstract or intellectual. The best example is reading: the letters you put together to form words are unimportant empirically (e.g., it doesn't matter how much color or what font is used for a printed letter), but combined they become signs for a reality they represent (e.g., the word *book*). Many words together convey a *meaning* and are thus intended to be understood by somebody. Yet *meaning* is an abstract thing just as any generalization (e.g., "society" or "life form"). Knowing such abstract things, however, seems to be different from knowing material objects: while material objects are in time, abstract objects are independent of it.

Some philosophers have argued that *all* of our knowledge derives from putting sensory information together: for them we encounter impulses that our mind then constructs into "things." The problem with this view is that it makes reality our *creation*. Instead of encountering *things*, we are in this view lonely minds that "reconstruct" the world. How problematic this is becomes obvious when you apply this theory to encountering fellow humans: this philosophy claims that we encounter this and that sensory impulse, and based on these impulses we construct that such and such must be a person. Yet is this really how we approach humans? Imagine somebody you love. Do you really encounter this person first as a body to which you add in your mind the characteristics "human," "person," "has dignity," and so forth? I rather think that we encounter other people *as persons* and not as a sum of their empirical parts (her height, weight, hair color, etc.). After all, each and every person's life begins with such a holistic encounter of one's parents: If a newborn child is left alone and has no "other" to care for and love her, she will die. The child recognizes her caretakers first, and only afterward does the world with its objects become interesting for her. The child does not register sensual impulses and then construct that behind the care she receives there must be a caretaker. Instead, the child recognizes the parent! Such an encounter, however, is not just sensory but also emotional and intellectual—it happens in multiple dimensions of our existence.[4]

Our world begins with the encounter of at least *one person*, and if we do not want to reduce human beings to mere *data* and lose the ability to defend the dignity of humans, then we have to hold on to a realistic, holistic knowledge of reality: we first encounter real things and persons, not pieces of information. Only once we step back from such spontaneous, holistic encounters and reflect on them can we identify parts and elements.

Knowledge is therefore much more than just an accumulation of information. You can do an easy experiment: Look up from your book and look straight ahead. What do you see? You know the objects you see exist although you only get a small fraction of data through your eyes to suggest they actually exist. I look at my computer and see behind it a green wall with many family pictures. In front of me is a bowl with cherries, and I assume my wife placed it here to remind me to eat healthy food. I smell nothing because the air conditioner is on. What my eyes receive are some data that suggest objects exist in front of me, but it is our mind that connects them to a holistic experience, builds up the perspective of a three-dimensional room, of my office desk and my dark green picture wall. Even without touching or eating the cherries I know they are there, because I have learned to trust my overall experience of reality. Even without taking the pictures from the wall, I know they have a backside (on which I usually pin a note of when the picture was taken). My mind does not receive any sensory data about this backside but "adds" to the impression it has received, because we encounter real *things* (which have a back, while the mere sensory impulse just shows me the front!) and not pieces of information. Simplistic theories that boil all knowledge down to sensory impulses eclipse these problems, and I therefore find them intellectually unsatisfying. To come back to the example of the human person: when I encounter a person, I immediately *recognize* personality and life.[5]

This chapter has tried to ask what knowledge is and explain how it differs from wanting or feeling. We have carved out a number of important characteristics of knowledge, such as intentionality, trust, truth, and the fact that knowledge is not limited to material objects but extends also to abstract things.

What we haven't done, however, is look at what knowledge *does*. When it arrives at a truth, it acquires the ability to state that things in mind and reality correspond to each other. What happens in the mind, however, is that knowledge somehow *reconstructs reality* there: we encounter something, and our mind re-creates it *in us* so that we "own" it. Naturally, such a reconstruction of the world is always fragmentary and in need of correction, but I see in it also a beacon of hope for humanity: Every day when we wake up, we make ourselves ready to encounter *the* world. Yet since every world *we* encounter will be *our* world, because we see it through *our* eyes and *our* mind, we can *change this world by changing ourselves*. My outlook on reality might not bring about the changes I would like to see, but perhaps it can attract others to see the world like I do. Thus knowledge prepares us to develop a stance toward the world as a whole, something many philosophers have called a *worldview*, a theory of how everything hangs together and belongs together. Many such worldviews are possible. Some construct them with God, some without, but they all rely on some kind of knowledge about the world.

3

The Power of Reason and Eternity

Rediscovering the power of human reason means also acknowledging how far it can go. In the previous chapter, I talked about humility and incompetence, but in this one I would like to highlight the astonishing feature of reason being able to reach toward timeless truths—namely, true intellectual knowledge that is not based on and is independent of empirical/measurable experience (weight, depth, height, etc.).

This is all the more important since the ability of reason to arrive at such intellectual knowledge is under attack today. One of the most common allegations is that reason is never able to grasp timeless truths because it changes according to the norms and expectations of a society. While such societal norms certainly change (e.g., women gained the right to vote), it does not follow that reason is therefore incapable of grasping *any* timeless, immutable truths. Many would say that this could only apply to mathematics and not to moral laws. Yet by throwing doubt on the ability of reason to find timeless truths, such critics seem to imply that the human mind is no different from that of other vertebrate animals and has no privileged access to an immaterial world. This of course eliminates the question about an immaterial soul!

Where Do We Find Laws?

I hope you and I will agree that scientific laws are necessary in order to understand nature. The first book on biology, *History of Animals*, was written by Aristotle almost twenty-five hundred years ago. It begins by classifying animals and grouping them according to characteristics. Later generations were able to formulate laws of biology. The same can be said of physics, chemistry, and so forth. Without the discovery of these laws of nature, we would not have the many amenities we daily enjoy. We wouldn't have the internet, cars, TV, modern medicine; we would be helplessly exposed to nature and its threats and unable to build the cities we have today. Perhaps we would be happier without all of that, but we would definitely live much shorter lives, we would be much more susceptible to infectious diseases and plagues, and our lives would be shaped by hard physical labor, like those in ancient civilizations. While we can see that the discovery of scientific laws has helped us in many ways, what is a law like Newton's law of inertia?

When we encounter *things* in this world, we realize that they have a location. For example, I am sitting *at my desk*, writing this book. Moreover, we perceive that things exist in a certain time and that everything material we know (e.g., our universe or ourselves) has a beginning and will at some point cease to exist. We also experience change; today I am healthy, but I might come down with the flu tomorrow. Last but not least, each thing is singular. I am sitting on *my* bike and not my brother's, even if it is the same brand and model. Let's compare this with the laws of nature!

Once we go through our list of characteristics, we will see that the laws of nature or math have *none* of these qualities. The reason for this is that laws are *universal* and not singular, are (usually) independent of time, do not change, are valid everywhere and not just in one place, and so forth. Think about it: it makes no sense to say that the *zero properties law*—which says that any number plus zero equals the original number—exists "in my school" or "only at noon," changes daily, or is not valid on the moon. It would be equally silly to say that Newton's law of inertia ("a body will remain in a state of rest or in a state of motion unless it is acted upon by an unbalanced force"[1]) is only valid at teatime or only valid in Europe.

A law is the same everywhere and at all times; it is universal and exists with necessity. Some might object and say that some of our laws, especially the ones in physics, only give us probabilities and are never fully *necessary*. That is true, but they inform us that something happens *necessarily* with this and that *probability* (e.g., that an apple is most likely to fall downward). So even here, we don't escape necessity.

Laws are never contingent like we are; *contingent* means that something may or may not be, and that it will cease to exist at some point. Laws, however, are *timeless*. But if laws are necessary and universal, while everything else we discover is finite and singular, they seem like ghosts: How can we as finite beings grasp something infinite? How are laws even possible? This is a question the scientist cannot help us answer; instead, it is the philosopher's job.

Laws Are Ghosts from Another World

With laws, the Polish philosopher Joseph Bochenski said, the timeless and eternal creep into our world, something "otherworldly."[2] Some philosophers have argued that since our mind is in essence immaterial and thus exists in a way similar to the way laws exist, it can recognize such "ghostly" things. It takes a ghost to catch a ghost, so to speak! Other philosophers felt very uncomfortable with this notion and consequently stated that laws are not really laws of the real world but rather produced through our mind by associating things with each other. At first glance that would make sense: you observe something, connect it to something else, and summarize your findings in a law. Yet if you state that laws are *created* by our minds and not "real," you have abandoned the idea of laws altogether. If there is no *real* law, how can we predict the speed of a falling body? If no *real* laws exist, why does the application of these allegedly "invented" laws work in everyday life? Why would we use these laws (e.g., for building a rocket or an airplane) if they were not reliable guides to *reality*? All these questions remain unanswered by those who claim that laws are merely the product of our mind but don't exist in reality.

Therefore, it seems to me much more reasonable to understand laws as indicators that certain things exist in this world *that are not physical and that have a different sort of existence*, to which our mind has privileged access. We can think about and discover these laws and formulate them inside our head. Yet if a surgeon opened up my skull, she would not find "laws" there but merely brain tissue, because the mind is not identical with matter. Laws and mind seem to share a common horizon: they are both *immaterial*, but unlike laws, our mind is finite and needs a time-bound body to function.

Laws of nature, mathematics, and the like are *discovered* by our mind and lifted out of the darkness of matter into the light of reason. We find them but do not create them or make them up. Things that exist in the material world, like my laptop, can be called *real*, while things whose existence we can only testify to with our minds, like the laws of math, we can call *ideal or abstract*.

You can easily imagine it with these examples: Think of the number forty-seven. Does the number forty-seven exist only when you or any other person thinks of it? If the world blew up and everyone died, no one would be around to think of the number forty-seven, but the number itself would still exist! Ideal things have an *odd* form of existence, about which philosophers have debated for two thousand years without ever coming to an agreement. Nevertheless, it is reasonable to call laws universals (see chap. 5 to clarify any questions that might have arisen from this chapter).

4

Knowing Yourself Is the Key to Logical Thinking

The search of the mind doesn't happen in a lifeless tank but inside of us. But what am I? Who am I? Perhaps you have experienced what the poet Jean-Paul Richter describes here: "One morning when I was still a child, I was standing on the threshold of the house looking to my left in the direction of the woodpile when suddenly there came to me from heaven like a lightning flash the thought: I *am a self*—a thought, which has never left me. I perceived *my self* for the first time and for good."[1] I don't remember such a single moment, but at some point, I became conscious of my own self and perceived myself as a living *unity*. Because I am a unity, I am different from everything else. I am my own being, and I am not my brother. I am different from the house I live in, and the food I eat does not make "me."

This "me" is an ongoing project. I make decisions that shape my life and who I will become. While much of my personality might be determined by my genes, I have the choice to mold myself into the person I want to be. In order to do that, however, I need to know *what* I want to become, or as Cicero, the ancient Roman politician and philosopher, said: "Above all . . . it has to be established who and what kind of person I wish to be . . . and this is the most difficult problem in the world."[2]

The Principle of Identity

Here one of philosophy's most important principles has its origin, the so-called *principle of identity*. The principle of identity states that a being is identical with itself. This may sound weird or superfluous, but I assure you it is not. We can know things because we recognize things as unities, as individual things. The best analogy I can think of is walking at night. Some ten years ago, I was a visiting professor at Princeton, and after a dinner party, I decided to walk home. It was a beautiful spring evening, but the neighborhood didn't have any streetlights. As the sun went down, it got very dark, and I tried to find my way home (in vain) until a car pulled up: "Ulrich, do you need a ride?" I don't think I was ever happier to see a friend stopping to give me a lift! Let's apply this analogy to the principle of identity: I cannot distinguish objects in complete darkness because I cannot perceive where one thing ends and the other begins. I need some light so that I can discern their boundaries and not become disoriented (or walk down a cul-de-sac!) Because I am "I," I can identify other things that are not myself and grasp their existence as separate units.

Becoming Mindful of Your Surroundings

The question of who you are is not just important as you move toward adulthood, but remains so throughout life. Remember that after seven years, every cell in your body has been replaced—but nevertheless you are not a different person. Some features might have changed; perhaps my face has more wrinkles, and I am no longer as fast a runner as I was, but I am fundamentally still the same person I was seven years ago. Some substance underneath the cellular changes remained identical. The fact that we even ask ourselves who we are sets us apart from all other animals. As far as we know, only human beings wonder "Who am I?" and try to find their place in society (albeit certainly influenced by instincts). Only humans have to develop a stance toward the world, while animals are largely controlled by their instincts. And since we are living organisms, we can conclude that the question about identity and thus consciousness of ourselves as a "self" is only found in living beings.

Life brings us in contact with the world outside our consciousness. When I sip my cup of coffee, I feel the shape of an object different from my body, a smell and taste that is not me. Yet how often do I attentively feel the handle between my fingers or relish the taste of this drink? Only if I become mindful of my surroundings will I really pay attention to influences on my body and self. I learn to appreciate myself as a point of stability in a sea of change and become more perceptive to external influences, as well as my reactions to them. When was the last time you paid attention to the surroundings of your workplace, its colors and shapes? How do you experience yourself when you encounter these? Such reasoning can make us *mindful* of the world around us and teach us to appreciate the small things in life while also empowering us to take control of our life. After all, only the person mindful of such influences is able to choose which one she allows to impact her life and which she deliberately rejects as harmful. All this would be impossible without the principle of identity, without the knowledge that "I am I," because I could not encounter anything as something different from me!

Objects Teach Us about Reality

We know the difference between ourselves and other objects, but if we want to know ourselves, we have to *objectify ourselves*. This means that we have to put the spotlight on our self in order to examine it. When we do that, one of the things we discover is that we *are*, that we *exist*. We only know things because they rise out of the dark abyss of nothingness, because they exist (see the analogy of a walk at night, above). The principle of identity demonstrates to us that existence is *utterly different from nonexistence*, that *to be* means to have a perfection that nonexistent things do not have. A principle that initially looked a bit odd has led us to think about the affluence and "luxury"[3] of our own existence.

Stretch out your hand and feel the object closest to you. In my case, it's a book lying on my table (my kids say I have way too many books). I can feel the surface of the old, worn dust jacket and smell a hint of pipe tobacco emerging from its pages because the previous owner was a heavy smoker. I see it is approximately 11 inches long, 8 inches wide, and 1.5 inches thick. What do you feel and experience right now? Perhaps a lamp, a laptop, or a desk? Whatever you feel and experience, it is a thing that you cannot manipulate with your mind. No matter how strongly you wish the lamp away or how much you would like to walk through the walls of your office, matter will resist you. Perhaps this sounds awfully silly to you, but I guarantee that it's not.

This experience of resistance demonstrates two important truths. First, there is a reality *outside my mind*—something that is *not me* (which is another application of the principle of identity). Second, this experience shows us that this *reality* has its own mind, so to speak, because it resists me and is independent from my mind. Perhaps the second truth sounds obvious to you, but since some philosophers have claimed that the world outside our mind does not exist, that we are brains in a tank (remember the movie *The Matrix*?), or that our mind brings the world into being, this experiment is crucial evidence that these philosophers got it wrong!

Yet don't think this is just a problem for philosophers—far from it! In our world, there are plenty of people who deny *realism*, which means that they deny that we can gain true knowledge of the real world. Instead of encountering the world and discovering it, they argue that reality should bend to whatever they want it to be. Or think of those who walk through life without any mindfulness for fellow human beings and their environment. They are so distracted by their search for wealth or security, or by staring at screens, that they effectively shield themselves from encountering reality on a more profound level. One can only hope they will one day delight in the liberating experience of *realism*!

Finding Relationships between Objects

So, if there exists a world outside our mind, the next big question is whether our mind has the potential to know something *true* about this world. Is this world intelligible and thus discoverable by reason? Can our mind turn toward *anything* in this world and acquire knowledge about it? Is our mind genuinely open to focus on anything it wants?

It certainly seems so. Even if we do not know what is inside a black hole, we can identify one and describe it to the best of our knowledge. That's what the ancient Greek philosopher Aristotle meant when he said that the soul, the core of our consciousness, *can become everything*.[4] It does not mean that it becomes the black hole we look at, but rather that everything that exists is intelligible and can be—to some extent—grasped by the mind. Our mind lifts what's intelligible out of an object (its *form*) and thus in a sense synthesizes or reconstitutes the object in the mind. It's important, though, to state that this does not mean that the mind makes an "image" of any sort; the intellectual form is a holistic way of getting to know an object (remember chap. 2!).

If our mind can intentionally focus on anything, could we also aim it at one of the riddles we all deal with in life—namely, relationships? Why not?! After all, we have thus far focused on individual things, so it might be helpful to now think about how things and persons relate to each other.

The world we experience is full of relationships. Some of them are built by nature and evolution (e.g., conscious life is related to the existence of carbon and oxygen), some by society and our own decisions (such as getting married). Have you ever asked yourself what you think about such relationships? For example, what is the relationship of my physical body and its diverse abilities to "the world"? What does *world* even mean?

When we dissect the term *world*, we discover a myriad of connections and relationships that we probably have never thought about. Identifying such things helps us to pinpoint, for example, common goods and values, or patterns of injustice.

By discovering relationships, we can spot things that we may have unconsciously pursued, obligations we feel bound by, dependency on others,[5] and much more. In short, we learn an awful lot about ourselves by putting the spotlight on the many relationships we have.

Nevertheless, we also learn through them about our immediate and wider surroundings. How do my life goals relate to those of my spouse? How does my lifestyle relate to the lifestyle of those in the developing world? How do my actions relate to the continuation of justice or injustice, the flourishing or decaying of the common good, to animals, plant life, and the environment?

Such questions often fall within the scope of ethics, or thinking about how to live the good life. Ethical systems that deny the principle of identity (and such exist) lose their claim to evaluate *any* relationship, because it is only through the principle of identity that we can identify relationships: only because I am a unit, a self, and different from others can I identify others with whom I enter a relationship. Without the principle, ethics would be lost.

Nothingness Is Your Invention

When we find a thing like a rock, we recognize it as a *being* in the world. It has real existence. Everything we discover is a being, even numbers (*ideal beings*), because we can only encounter things that have some kind of existence or being. Things that do not exist, whether in the physical world or in our mind, are nonbeings. While rocks, trees, and numbers exist independently from us and are part of the physical world, "nothingness" does not.

The idea of *nothing* is only possible because we have grasped the idea of being; only when we negate it do we arrive at *nothing*. The principle of identity also sheds light on this. All that is, exists (*is*), and only our mind constructs the idea of nothingness by negating being. Now, don't fall into the trap of thinking that "nothingness," as it is sometimes portrayed in science fiction or a fantasy book (e.g., in Michael Ende's *The Neverending Story*), is a gigantic black hole—because that is again *something* (dark matter, possibly). Nothing is absolutely *nothing*. We can only *imagine* it; it is not *real*.

While *nothing* is the negation of being, we also use simpler negations, such as when we deny a certain characteristic of a thing—for example, we can imagine *nonwhite* snowflakes. But even such simple negations cannot be understood by animals because they rely on concepts, which the active intellect lifts from reality. Animals, however, do not have concepts (at least as far as we know).

Negation is therefore something *only* human beings are capable of conceiving. Another difference between humans and animals, some philosophers have claimed, is that humans can actively desire "nothingness" and the negation of meaning—by suicide, for example. Try to think of any other living being that could aim at nothingness, be it animal or plant. None are able to do it, I think. But neither can humans! Even if we want to do *nothing*, we have to *objectify* nothingness. We have to give it some kind of *being* in order to "intend" it. A person who denies all meaning and desires nothingness could commit suicide, but even that is an act; it's something very concrete that you desire. Even contemplating nothingness as the great "engine" for one's life (nihilism) only works by secretly smuggling *being* into nothingness, making it appear as "something." It is the great tragedy of human life that what empowers us to discover the secrets of the universe also contains the seeds of destruction: because we can conceive of nothingness, we can be tempted to negate order and meaning by choosing self-destruction.[6]

But I do not want to end on such a pessimistic note. If you look closer, you will realize that even if we decide to embrace nihilism, we cannot escape meaning. The moment you try to convey to others that the meaning of life is nothingness, you turn nothing into something, which is contradictory. So even when we deny all meaning, we cannot escape meaning—and therefore neither should you! Life is too wonderful and too adventurous to give up on it. Never forget that this world is a better place because of you—because you exist!

5

Good Thinking Is Always Focused

T he other day, I couldn't help staring at the ceiling above my fireplace because I saw a water stain there and realized my roof was leaking. Finding the *reason* for a roof leak can be nerve-racking, and perhaps you have gone through something similar. Replacing the chimney flashing was one thing, sleeping well after the repair another. For days afterward, I couldn't get the thought of a leaking roof out of my head even though the repair had been done properly. Sometimes I can't fall asleep because many different thoughts are going through my head. Usually, I enjoy thinking about things, particularly when I'm reading or writing, but not when I am trying to rest. Using philosophy to sort out what thinking is, however, helped me to better understand what is going on in my head and find strategies to deal with it. By identifying the difference between real thoughts and emotions, I realized that I often let irrational beliefs (see chap. 14) influence me.

My Thinking Is Not Identical with Brain Events

What is a thought, though, and what makes it different from a dream or a feeling? I couldn't tell you anything about physical brain functioning because I am not a physician. Such a person could tell you which lobe of the brain is responsible for what kind of thinking or how anxiety or drugs can alter our perception. All these mechanical and chemical interactions are researched by the natural/medical sciences and psychology. Philosophy, however, is interested in *what* thinking is. What makes a thought a thought? And that I can attempt to clarify.

Thinking happens *within me*. That's a good starting point, because we have already found out quite a bit about the "I," the principle of identity, and our consciousness. If thinking happens *in me and by me*—I am doing the thinking—then it must have a first-person perspective (see chap. 10). *I* have thoughts and only *I* can articulate them. An observer does not have access to my thoughts (and even if I share them with him, they—just like sentences about feelings—are already objectified). This "I" who thinks is more than just a blob of tissue; it is a *mind*. Nevertheless, the mind is not totally independent from brain tissue (see chaps. 9 and 10) because we know that we cannot think without our brain.

Whenever I think something (*mind*), an event occurs in my brain. Consequently, some have assumed that brain events cause the mind or produce it. Yet the fact that two things happen simultaneously does not mean that you can infer that one is necessarily caused by the other. Moreover, how can something *material* (brain event) cause something *immaterial* (my thought)? Until today, no convincing argument has been produced for how the brain allegedly produces consciousness![1]

Although researchers have found that each thought corresponds to certain neuron activities in the brain, what we *experience* (first-person or I-perspective) are *not* neuron impulses but *things*: trees, persons, pain, joy, and so forth. These are fundamentally different from neuron interactions—they have a *different reality*, because the tree you see in your garden does not simply enter your brain but is somehow mirrored in it (I called this an *intellectual form*, if you remember), represented, thereby becoming an object of your mind. In your mind, it has an existence of its own and is no longer dependent on the source of the sensory image in your garden.

Thinking Is Not Feeling

Not everything that happens in my mind is a thought. Think of pain! When I sprain my ankle, I feel pain; it happens to *me*, and I am aware of it, but I don't "think" it. Nobody would say that—and there is a reason for it: pain is a *passive* experience, it *happens* to you. Thoughts are different because they have an *active* nature.

When I perceive something, like a tree, I am more or less passive, but when I think about something, my mind is active and directs its attention to it. It *intends* something, zooms in on an object, focuses on it and aims at knowing it. That's what we do when we think: we actively zoom in on certain objects (like I did with my leaking roof) and make them present to our consciousness.

Thinking, therefore, also differs from *imagination*. When I imagine things, I only form an image in my mind of something but do not examine what the essence of this image means. I can imagine unicorns without really *thinking* about unicorns; when I do that, I imagine a picture, but I leave out the intellectual form of unicorns—namely, how they would exist and why and where. Mere imagination is a bit like the cartoon version of a great movie because it leaves out reality. If you don't believe me, try it out yourself and see whether there is a difference between seeing a car, imagining a car, and thinking about a car.

When I think about the roundness of a table, I direct my attention not just to a table but also to something else. The table is the object, but its roundness is a state that exists *on* the object. Objects can be *real*, such as bodies that cause sense perceptions (e.g., my desk), or they can be *abstract* or *ideal*, such as numbers or geometric figures.

Thus the first characteristic of thinking seems to be that it aims at objects (*intention*) and that thinking *connects these intentional objects to form state-ments.*[2] Out of the intentional objects "table" and "roundness" my thinking, which I can also call *reasoning*, produces the statement: "The table is round."

If thinking "aims" at something, is it ever satisfied once it has hit its target? It seems that our urge to think only comes to an end when our thought has reached its goal, like when an arrow hits its target. You can try this out yourself by trying to think of a red car while looking at a blue one; repeat the statement "the car is red" a few times in your mind while you stare at the blue car. It will be an odd experience because it is difficult for your mind to reconcile the sensory experience of "blue car" with the wrong description of "red car" that you are giving it. Your mind rebels because you do not allow it to hit the target. Your mind is never in neutral!

Thinking Abstract Things

Let's take this a step further: Have you ever wondered how objects enter your mind? Why do you even think about them? Some objects seem to "swing" into our consciousness, without us searching for them. They attract our attention, just like old friends we see on the street and suddenly feel the urge to greet.[3]

The other possibility is that we intend to make something the goal of our thinking. Let's say you want to think about social justice. You don't start by repeating the words over and over to yourself like a parrot. After all, thinking wants to *understand* and find intellectual forms. Thus, you first look at the adjective *social* and then at the noun *justice*, asking yourself what these two entail. In a next step you can reason whether the combination of these words constitutes a new concept or whether the adjective merely describes the noun.

Yet how is our brain able to think about something as abstract as justice? After all, our brain needs impressions from the sensory world, and there is no empirical object called "justice" that we can touch or see (apart from the allegorical figure we see in front of courthouses!).

This is the problem of *universals*. It is one of the most hotly debated philosophical questions of all time. Universals are abstract concepts such as "justice" or "social." They are higher categories that allow us to subsume many things under them: for example, we put equal treatment, the right to an attorney, humane prisons, and much more under the term *justice*. Nevertheless, it's always we who come up with such classifications. We put things into certain categories and create the words for them. That does not mean, however, that we invent them. Instead, when I *think* of "justice," I conceive an *intellectual form in my mind of what it entails*, and I lift this universal, abstract concept out of a multitude of other experiences. I "find" it there, Aquinas would say.[4]

The method used to come up with such concepts is called *abstraction*. The intellect works through abstraction and peels away layers of meaning from our original sensory experiences until it finds the *intelligible form* underneath, which it then puts into words.

Instead of "justice," let's use an example from the sensory world: a thing used by humans to sit on is a chair. The *intellectual form* is what makes a chair possible and defines it as such a thing. Such a form gives a thing its unity and determination. Thus it must never be misunderstood for mere physical shape. In fact, form does *not* mean any kind of material shape—it is entirely abstract. Nevertheless, the form is connected to a physically existing thing but not identical with it. For example, if I use a chair as a piece of modern art, it still has the shape of a chair but has gained a new, additional (and artificial) form. We also find such intellectual forms in living things, in which they are more substantial: a living rabbit has an intellectual form that rabbit stew does not.[5] Or to look at another example, imagine you encounter a beautiful animal that people are riding, but you have never seen such a creature before. You ask, "What is that?" and are told, "This is a horse." You have received a name, which only if you understand its meaning becomes a *concept*. For this process of understanding or insight, however, you have to ask yourself *what* "horse" entails, especially what its *necessary* characteristics are. For Aristotle and Thomas Aquinas, this means focusing the spotlight of our active mind (*intellectus agens*)[6] onto the impressions we have received from seeing the animal. The mind lifts an *intelligible form* out of these impressions and constitutes a concept. A universal is born. Nevertheless, such is *not* a creation of our mind in the same way a poem is; it is not a "social construct," but, like a law, is something that we *found in an object* and *put into words*. It is a mirror of reality!

You may wonder why anyone would care, right? It may sound like a problem only philosophers would waste time on, but I assure you, denying universals has drastic consequences. Scientists make such enormous progress because they talk to each other in a worldwide community. They rely on the power of the mind to form and use concepts, to identify the "whatnesses" of things. Without concepts, every one of them would have her own language, and communication would be impossible. Despite this obvious truth, many scholars in the humanities, particularly those working on language and grammar, have abandoned the idea that we can find common, rationally communicable characteristics of things and talk about them. In postmodernism, for example, the search for a common nature of "things" is completely abandoned, because truth is regarded as relative. Nobody can say any longer what the "nature of a human being" is because "truth" is what you make it. Everything has become a "construct," which is a fancy word for something invented. For postmodernists, concepts are merely mirroring the conventions of language. People have agreed that certain words denote a certain concept, but they are not words that truthfully inform you about reality. Consequently, postmodernists construct their own reality. Yet, by doing so, they commit a performative self-contradiction: by stating that it is impossible to flesh out the nature of something, they make a claim about the nature of things!

Such thinking threatens the very existence not only of human rights but also of our free world. People can think whatever they want, but that cannot mean that one should let a dangerous philosophy rule college classrooms and schools. A person who rejects postmodernism does not claim that a particular concept of human nature is exhaustive or covers every aspect of reality, but rather that it is an abstract truth that is accessible and applicable to everyone.[7] Abandoning the idea of finding out the truth of things makes communication with each other, listening and understanding, impossible. And I fear that our society has reached this point, yet without addressing the underlying philosophical problem. Rejecting our intellect's ability to find the whatness of things, however, is a self-defeating philosophy: Its claim that we cannot grasp the nature / intelligible form / whatness of something is *already* a truth claim about this whatness. Moreover, the claim is formulated in words you and I can understand and thus presupposes universal concepts. This theory is not self-applicable; it is a bit like the philosopher who claimed the world outside his mind did not exist but who drank water during his lecture. He could not live his contradicting philosophy—otherwise he would have had to die of thirst and remain silent forever.

Therefore, knowing a realist philosophical approach remains so important in our world. I find it attractive especially because on the one hand, it pushes me to encounter the world, but on the other hand, it acknowledges the active part of our intellect in discovering the riddles of the universe. Instead of one-sidedness, it is holistic!

Order for Our Thinking: Genus and Species

In order to acquire any knowledge, we get to know particular things first and then we construct concepts or universals for them by abstraction. Aristotle found that there are only five ways in which we can talk about all beings, whether they are animals, humans, rocks, or ghosts, with only one exception: God.[8] When I read them for the first time in a philosophy seminar in college, they were like a revelation to me. My confused and easily distracted ADHD brain had finally found a way to create order in my life and world! The feeling of assurance I gained from these five ways never faded; it accompanies me wherever I go and whatever I undertake.

The five *predicables*, as the philosophical tradition calls them, help us on the way to abstraction because they instruct us about what kind of layers we have to consider peeling away. The first predicable is that of *genus*: When we determine the genus of a thing, we list all the characteristics this thing has in common with others. In the case of the horse, we can say with certainty that the genus would be an animal. A horse, like a beaver or a bird, is an animal life-form.

The second level is the *species*. A species is a universal idea that expresses the *whole* nature of a thing, and it is subsumed *under* the genus. This *predicable* probably takes the longest to determine. Many of the mistakes I've made in my thinking have happened here, usually because I was not careful enough, didn't pay attention to all of the details, and arrived at the wrong classification. Therefore, I have learned to be especially patient when I have to classify species in my own work, and this kind of thinking is just as tough and demanding as any physical work would be! Our example of a horse is easy, because we all know a bit about horses, but think of some things we do not know well and yet have to describe. The species of a horse would be something like *herbivore mammal*, expressing its essence (and as I said earlier, this is never a fully exhaustive definition!). You will immediately realize that this essence is shared by a number of other animals, such as camels or donkeys. Therefore, there has to be another layer of classification that answers the question of what makes a horse different from the *other* herbivore mammals.

A horse has *an odd number of toes and a special stomach*—so we could put this down as the third level, called the *specific difference* within a species. By naming this difference, we are able to flesh out characteristics that also help us understand other species better—for example, carnivorous reptiles.

The fourth level of classification pertains to the *proper* or *essential* characteristics an object has. In the case of the horse, we would have to identify characteristics necessary to understand what "horse" means, such as the ability to sprint fast and the potential to be tamed for human use.

Only the fifth point of classification names *accidental* properties, which are characteristics that an object just happens to have but does not necessarily have. For example, horses can have spotted fur.

Having a system of classification such as this not only enables biologists to create a tree of life, understanding commonalities and differences among the many different species on our planet, but also enables our thinking to be clear and focused. Predicables empower the human mind to discover the world and *structure* it rationally, whether for research, business models, or other things.

Our Mind Is Not Inventing "Justice"

So far so good. Now we know how we arrive at concepts or universals that represent real things in the world. Let's get back to our abstract example of "justice." *What* do we think about when we think about justice? The beauty of Aristotle's theory is that it shows us how human minds discover the *intellectual forms* in things but do not invent them. Such discovery is accessible to everyone and therefore has a wonderful egalitarian aspect to it.

Nevertheless, some philosophers deny that such forms exist and rather argue that our experiences create an image in our mind to which we give abstract names like "justice." The problem I have with this theory is that it reduces universals such as justice to figments of our own personal imagination. They are no longer a reality that all people have access to, but relative to the beholder. I find this not only intellectually but also ethically unconvincing.

Moreover, I doubt that we have an image in our mind for every abstract concept such as justice. If I think, for example, of a chiliagon, which is a polygon with one thousand sides, my mind does not construct an exact image but merely a big polygon. The polygon in my imagination only mirrors the intellectual form behind it, which has exactly one thousand sides. Thus, the form influences the image and not vice versa. Now let's do the same experiment with the example of "justice." What is my image and what is your image when you think of the abstract term *justice*? I think of a courtroom with an old judge; you might think of scales or something like that. If so, we both have different images in our mind when we think of this abstract concept. However, that does not prove we have a different idea of justice. After all, why did you and I associate our different images with the idea of "justice"? If my mind has no clue what the essence of justice is, its *whatness*, how could we associate it with such images? It seems there must be a bridge between the images of justice and the idea of justice, which the critic cannot explain, and with his silence his theory also fades away. The intellectual form we have discovered allows us to create an image, but not the other way around! This shows us that humans can have varying images for abstract concepts, while the same intellectual form or *whatness* of this concept underlies those images: your image of scales expresses the same intellectual form of "justice" that my image of the wise judge does.

This should also evince how problematic it is to talk about abstract ideas *changing* over time. It is not so much the universal that changes but rather its application. The idea of "dignity" is, I dare say, at its root the same in our culture as in others. What differs is how it is applied in concrete circumstances such as in laws.

This is again more than mere philosopher's talk, because it proves that we can and must find out the *whatness* of things.

Some individuals might claim that we should not waste our time thinking about such abstract terms but should instead think about things in the real world, things we can touch, feel, and smell. Yet we can only get to the bottom of things if we *abstract*. After all, the terms "real world" and "climate" were found by abstraction! Giving up the idea of accurate abstract knowledge opens the door to the destruction not just of ethics but also of the human intellect. Wherever abstract thinking becomes devalued, reasoning is replaced by the expression of emotions and manipulation. And such anti-intellectualism is always how a tyranny begins.

The Tools of Thinking Are Analysis and Synthesis

It is important to shed some light on the two main ways of thinking, *analysis* and *synthesis*. In Greek, *analyein* means to loosen something up or unravel it. When we analyze an object in our mind, we "abstract" from it certain characteristics—we pull the characteristics off, layer by layer, like peeling an onion. By doing so, we see what constitutes the object and what the underlying substance is. For example, when I analyze "school," I have to find out what school entails. I pull off the layer of "my school" first (the here and now, the *accidental*) and try to find out what school in *general* is. By doing so, I discover that I can peel away the idea that school must be a building, because in the most general terms, it's really an institution. At the end of my unraveling, I arrive at the *intelligible form* of what school is, an abstract representation for it in my mind. It is intelligible because anyone with the powers of reason can examine my thought process and come to the same *form*. When I *synthesize* things, I put such forms together, connect and combine them, which is how most of our knowledge comes about.[9]

We only arrive at knowledge by forming *judgments*. Objects such as the tree in my front lawn are present to us, but only judgments are true or false. Judgments are also *intentional*, like "My house is green." Even if we paint the house *tomorrow* with a different color, the truth value of the sentence I just uttered remains valid for *today*—truth has no real relation to time. Truth is beyond time and states that what we say corresponds to the state of affairs.

A judgment applies truth to *beings*. In a judgment you connect different elements; for example, in the simple sentence "This tree is green," you connect the *subject* "tree" through the copula "is" with the *predicate adjective* "green." It is a judgment that you pronounce and you are convinced of, and it represents the reality of the intellectual form "green tree" in your mind. If the tree is dead and has no green on its branches, then the judgment is false. Judgment therefore necessarily rests on examining "evidence" and interpreting it correctly (namely, whether the tree is really green).[10]

One of the most exciting and yet difficult parts of reasoning is forming *conclusions*, which are the consequences of judgments. By connecting a series of judgments, we build in our mind something like the chain of a necklace. The last link, the latch that connects the beginning of the chain with the end and thus makes it a proper necklace, is the *conclusion*. It is what locks it all together. The puzzling thing about the conclusion is that the mind arrives at it by using judgments as *premises*. This is somewhat mystifying because something *new* comes into existence in the conclusion, some new knowledge, and yet somehow this new knowledge was invisibly entailed in the premises. The mind, just like with the universals we encountered above, has the power to lift the new knowledge out of these premises. It discovers it by extracting it from the premises!

Just as there are many kinds of necklace latches, there are also different types of conclusions, which are called *syllogisms*. For the most basic form of a syllogism, we can use this example: Premise 1 is the judgment "All birds have wings." Premise 2 is the judgment "All chickens are birds." The conclusion must be, therefore, "All chickens have wings." This is important because the two premises do not allow the mind the freedom to conclude whatever it desires, but rather force it to build the exact latch that makes a perfect chain. If the premises are correctly stated, then the conclusion necessarily follows.[11]

This, however, does not mean that the conclusion is true! You could have a perfectly correct syllogism that is nevertheless false, as is the case if one or two of the premises are false. A syllogism is only true if all the premises or prior judgments are true. That's why one calls syllogisms either *valid* (if the conclusion follows with necessity) or *invalid* (if there is a formal mistake in one of the elements or premises or in the conclusion). An example of a valid conclusion that is nevertheless false is as follows: Premise 1 states, "All Americans are philosophers." Premise 2 states, "Tom Brady is an American." The conclusion "Tom Brady is a philosopher" is validly drawn but still false because one of the premises is false. Such conclusions are called *fallacies*.[12] To sum it up, reasoning with a syllogism is a bit like making sausages. The end product is only as good as the material that goes into the meat grinder; if you follow the laws of logic, your conclusion will be valid, and if your premises are true, then your conclusion will be too.[13]

In the world of business, politics, and courtrooms, many are trained in syllogistic thinking, but they often use it to deceive others. They present you with premises that appear to be true and conclusions that seem undoubtedly correct, but once you examine them carefully, you will often see that they were drafted to hide factual inconsistencies. It is easy to be deceived by such things because they are cleverly expressed and are designed to manipulate our emotions, and the listener often has no time for fact-checking, which is why such flaws usually go undetected. Therefore, knowing the basic rules of good logical thinking, of identifying faulty syllogisms, is necessary not just for the philosopher but for every citizen. If more people knew about such logic and how to apply it, they would be better able to protect themselves from false advertising about things like reverse mortgages, for instance, and better able to detect when others are trying to take advantage of them.

Beware of Bad Comparisons and Analogies

One form of synthetic thinking is the comparison. We've all used one before. For instance, when we bought a new family van, my wife and I sat down and made a list of all the features we would need and then looked around at the different models on the market to see which one fit the bill. Then we compiled fact sheets and put them on our kitchen table in order to recognize similarities and differences between the car models.

The act of comparing things is crucial for gaining knowledge. It is so deeply ingrained in us that it has become a habit, especially in professions that could not work without comparisons. Imagine, for example, an employee in charge of buying merchandise: she has to compare the prices and quality of the products so that her orders leave a decent profit margin for her employer. Think of a historian, who has to constantly compare situations of the past, or a teacher, who must constantly assess which methodology works best in the classroom. Even though comparison is a widely used operation of the mind, most people do not do it well! In fact, we often make basic mistakes, especially when we use comparisons outside our areas of knowledge. So then, what does a good comparison entail?

Like with all other operations of the mind, comparisons are done by persons. So we have to constantly be aware of the prejudices or agendas that influence our comparisons. Our perspective can taint not just the *value* but also the *validity* of our comparison. All too often, we get carried away by our emotions and we compare, in a moment of anger or passion, things that do not belong together. I often see this on social media when a person or group is compared to Hitler. People identify something as evil and dangerous, perceive a vague similarity, and pull the "This is just what Hitler did!" card out of their hat. As a historian and a German, I can tell you that 99 percent of these comparisons are not only false but ludicrous. Likewise, I often hear "This is Marxism!" when most of the time the person uttering that statement has no idea what Marxism is (or, better, *was*), and the described policy or action has no reasonable connection to that ideology. That's why the advice of the first-century Roman historian Tacitus to take a step back in the moment of passion to clear one's head (*sine ira et studio*) is timeless!

The next step toward making a good comparison is identifying what belongs to it and what does not. *We distinguish and discern.* In most cases, we don't have to compare every quality of an object with every quality of another object to form an adequate comparison. We can put a small number of qualities of various objects next to each other in order to see whether they differ.

This operation demands two steps: First, it requires *attention* from us, since we have to focus on a number of differences. We can use our knowledge of species, genus, and specific difference as well as the categories (form, quantity, quality, etc.) to spot them.[14] Second, once we have recognized the differences between things, we can take the next step and see w*hether different things have the same qualities*. For example, when I am shopping for new tires, I am mostly interested in safety and longevity, so I compare a number of models accordingly and disregard the other characteristics.

The real problem, though, is that we often compare things that should not be compared because their similarities are only *superficial* or because we do not really have a good *grasp* of what we are looking for. If I want to know what kind of wheel is better for getting around in the snow slush on Midwestern roads in the winter, I should not compare a wagon wheel to a car tire. If I do it, then I have focused merely on a common *essential characteristic* (round and used to move an object) that I have found in both, but I have neglected their *substantial differences* (rubber versus wood; mechanical versus animal powered). Thus my comparison will be invalid, because I should have focused on comparing different car tires to each other.

Sometimes, however, we seem to do just that—namely, comparing things without recognizing their substantial differences.

As easy as comparisons often look, good ones require careful consideration. We often fail to see differences because we are unaware of our *hidden biases*. We might proudly proclaim that we want to know the truth, but that does not mean that we are unbiased in our search. In fact, more often than not, something in our mind keeps twisting our research into directions that merely confirm such unacknowledged, often subconscious biases. A good researcher therefore constantly has to watch out for these pitfalls and to use extreme caution. Otherwise he will arrive at faulty results. Introspection—that is, trying to shed light on one's own ideas and prejudices—is probably the hardest thing to do, but, again, philosophy will help one learn to do such scrutiny methodically. One of the easiest ways to avoid confirmation bias in comparisons (which is only one of many mental operations for which confirmation bias is possible) is to write down the qualities you discovered and force yourself *not* to make any comparison until you have identified some *substantial differences* between the objects you compare.

Even more difficult is what philosophers call *analogy*. Analogies compare relationships to each other and express that two or more things are *alike in some respect but dissimilar in others*. Some have aptly described analogy as the tool describing the *shades of likeness*.

When we use the same word to describe two different objects, we can either use it *univocally* (identical use; e.g., when we use "person" for me and you) or *equivocally* (different; e.g., when we use the word *cup* in a coffee shop and a football locker room). Yet there is a third option—namely, when we use the same word to describe things that are partially similar but also (often overwhelmingly) different. This latter, third way is called *analogical*.

You use the word *excellent* to describe your job performance, but you use the same adjective to characterize your gym membership. Both share a quality that justifies your use of the term, but your job performance and your gym membership are vastly different. Analogies are often proportional, so that one side of the comparison has a higher degree or proportion than the other. A classic example of this is the relationship between God (if such an entity exists) and human beings. If we describe both as *being*, then we understand that there is a commonality between them, because both exist. Yet if we dig deeper, we will find that if God exists, "he" exists with necessity, while human beings can exist or not exist (they are *contingent*)—their "hold" on being is less than God's. Both share *being* but in differing degrees or proportions.[15] (Although God transcends gender, the Christian tradition uses gendered pronouns to metaphorically express the relationships within the Trinity, which I follow here.)[16]

Analogies are important for all kinds of conclusions. In fact, much of our knowledge is built on conclusions from analogy. We find that if several objects—let's call them a, b, c, and d—have the same characteristics x and y, then they also have z in common. This is only correct if the characteristics or properties are essential. Moreover, my conclusion will be stronger if I can identify more such analogous commonalities.

Analogous and inductive conclusions are therefore related, and they are especially important in the natural sciences. An *induction* is a conclusion that is formed by observing objects—for example, I have observed many times in the past that the sun rises each morning, and thus I conclude that it will rise tomorrow. Of course, such *inductive reasoning* has deeper implications and problems, but that would lead us too far away from our discussion. *Deductions*, on the other hand, come about when I conclude from a general or universal statement the truth about a singular object. For example, if I know for sure that all birds lay eggs and I observe a wren outside my house, I can safely conclude from the first statement that wrens lay eggs. Obviously, deductions can also be faulty, especially if at least one of the presuppositions is false.[17]

Becoming aware of how our judgments are structured; of whether our conclusions are drawn from analogy, induction, or deduction; and of whether we make proper comparisons or analogies helps us to not only avoid flaws in our logic but also acknowledge a deeper truth behind it. Human minds are fallible, and we constantly make mistakes. Perhaps this insight will help us to be humbler in our conversations with each other, help us to be more patient with others (and ourselves) when they (and we) make mistakes, and compel us to be more precise in our expressions, using good comparisons, analogies, and logic.

6

Critical Thinking

I read a tweet this past spring that said, "Smoking Can Prevent COVID-19 Infection." It was about a medical study that had been conducted in Israel. While it is true that nicotine kills the virus, the study was not at all suggesting that anyone should take up smoking in order to fight the spread of the illness. Yet people often retweet or repeat comments they like without thinking about the entire background or context in which they were made. This is what makes fake news possible but also dangerous. Another example is income-tax scams: every year, thousands of people fall for bogus IRS phone calls threatening litigation unless they hand over their social security number and bank information.

In order to avoid being deceived, you have to be able to think critically. After all, critical thinking is the biggest enemy of fake news, credulity, and gullibility. Yet what is it and how is it achieved?[1]

When my oldest son began to inquire about which college to attend, dozens of advertisements arrived at our house. All of them promised to instill in him the "tools of critical thinking," but none explained what they meant by that. I found that frustrating. The adjective *critical* has its origin in the Greek verb *krinein*, which means "to discern." Being critical in this sense does not mean being judgmental, but rather trying to determine whether something is true.[2] Such discernment is done in a deliberate manner, in which information is evaluated and interpreted according to specific, reasonable criteria. I am not claiming that this description is exhaustive, but it is sufficient for continuing our meditation on what makes one a critical thinker.

Be Active and Not Passive

Philosophers tend to forget the active and personal side of critical thinking. They focus so much on technicalities, such as judgments pressed into the language of formal equations, that they lose the search for wisdom that is (or should be) at the heart of the philosophical enterprise. Such tools are certainly helpful, but if you make them the core of your philosophy, you have turned them into an ugly idol.

Instead, I focus on the starting point of critical thinking—namely, on a mind that desires to know. *Desire* is the key word here! If you don't really want to know or care enough about the truth of things, you will always be stuck on the surface. You sometimes see this at the meetings of professional academics: They enjoy winning sophisticated arguments in journals read by only a handful of people, but they are no longer *desiring to know*. Their intention is merely recognition and fame.[3]

Critical thinking is also first and foremost an *active endeavor*. It is never *passive*. If you just receive information, you might write a flawless, logically argued paper, but your heart will never be in it because you have never actively engaged with the material. Such passive learning is still the most common teaching technique in business schools and college campuses; it is the lecture method, where the student sits and quietly takes notes. Yet study after study has proven that only when we are exposed to *experiential learning and discussion*, when we are personally involved, do we learn *actively*. This is important because active learning allows us to truly appropriate knowledge instead of merely storing information in our heads. The best advice I can give you is to search for your *intellectual passions*, find out what questions drive you, and then have the courage to explore them![4]

Desire for *knowledge*, though, is different from the hunger for *information*. There is nothing wrong with desiring to possess information, but when we desire to know, we aspire to a more *profound* familiarity (see chap. 1) with the object. Such familiarity allows the critical thinker to evaluate and integrate new pieces of information into her bigger frame of knowledge. This not only allows for growth but also enables knowledge to mature into wisdom.

Critical thinking, however, is also the hard work of an *individual*. It manifests our autonomy and independence—our ability to come to our own judgments. Therefore, as a critical thinker, I have to try to break free from societal expectations and prejudices. I have to liberate my mind from preconceived ideas that might cloud my investigation.

Cutting Through Nonsense

Only once I am a fully active, critical thinker can I weigh and evaluate pieces of information properly. Such interpretation involves statements and statistics but also graphs and images. Churchill supposedly said once, "I only trust the statistics I have manipulated myself." Whether he actually said it or not, this quotation reminds us that information is hardly ever *raw*; it has usually already been *somehow* filtered. The critical thinker therefore has to find out what filters have been applied, so that she can make her own judgment. For example, if you are examining a graph depicting the declining number of illiterate people in the US, you should ask what methodology the researchers used to arrive at their numbers. What is their working definition of literacy? Does it merely mean the ability to read words? Does it include the ability to write as well? Does it include the faculty to understand complex sentences and images? Or, to say it more simply, you have to find out what the basic principles are that led to these numbers. Let me give you another example from my work as a historian. In the eighteenth century, monastic vocations steadily declined. Consequently, many historians concluded that religious practice also declined during that period and that the monastic lifestyle had lost its attraction. They did not, however, ask whether the state laws that prohibited young people from entering monasteries had anything to do with these statistics. Well, of course they did! And once I realized this, I was able to reject the conclusion of my peers and form a better one.[5]

By asking such questions, the critical thinker also *differentiates* real scientific/academic claims from *pseudoscience*. One of the most striking examples for me as a German is the denial of the Holocaust. I once met a person who tried to explain to me, based on the claims of an infamous British author, that no one was gassed in Auschwitz. Such people of course claim that "evidence" is on their side. Thus in order to refute them or to understand them better, we have to look at some of their basic strategies.

If you look more closely at such outrageous *conspiracy claims*, you will see that they always work the same way. Historical methods, although rigorously tested and used for calculating the number of victims or establishing the use of gas chambers for mass murder, are rejected, because the findings do not fit these people's worldview. Then they invent a theory to explain the facts anew.

The problem with this and all other such conspiracy theories is that they are never based on serious, rigorous scholarship. Instead, they work with half-digested methodologies founded on anecdote, credulity, and bad logic.

A critical thinker will not only understand the methods of the historian but also weigh them properly. By doing so, she will realize that the evidence for the Holocaust is so overwhelming that a few tiny problems here and there do not in the least justify its total denial or its downplaying. The critical thinker knows the criteria for good evidence and how to integrate evidence into a bigger theory, whereas the conspiracy theorist is unable to assess evidence correctly and thus places flimsy findings above well-established facts.[6]

You Know What Is Good Evidence

When you weigh information, you have to know what kind of evidence it was based on. You have to know whether the elements of a claim are true.

I have met people who believe the world is only six thousand years old. When I ask about what evidence they have for this, I always get two answers: (1) it is stated in the Bible (*evidential claim*), and (2) all of the scientific data that tell us the earth is older is false (*denial of opposing evidence*). I will not even begin criticizing the first statement (although much could be said about that)[7] but will rather tackle the second one. Denial of opposing evidence is a strategy that inoculates the person making the claim against all counterevidence. Whatever data you could bring in from astrophysics and biology is instantly dismissed because these sciences cannot explain this or that small detail of creation (yet). As you can see, the strategy is the same as with the Holocaust denier above: because a small portion of data cannot be explained by a theory, one dismisses the theory as a whole, because another theory fits better with one's worldview. I have friends who believe such claims about evolution, and while I love them dearly, I am convinced they are uncritical: they are not open to scientific truth (and of course they cannot see that religious and scientific truths do not conflict with each other because they belong to two different realms of meaning).[8]

This should also remind us of the importance of how evidence is collected and arranged. The critical thinker has to be on the lookout for pseudoscientists, who construct arguments using *counterfeit* evidence. They carefully pick data that fit their agenda and draw highly improbable/inaccurate conclusions, dismissing all contrary evidence before even engaging with it.

It is important to know about the methodology that various researchers use to collect and analyze information so that you can better determine whether it has been obtained properly, especially if you are not an expert. For example, I am a trained historian and theologian, but I do not know how to approach art history or music history, so whenever I have to engage with it, I make sure to ask my colleagues if I assessed the evidence correctly and made good use of their methods.

In the time and age of the internet, one has access to a variety of sound information but also myriad conspiracy theories and charlatans. One way to discern the good from the bad is to look to trusted institutions of knowledge, to standard handbooks and encyclopedias, to experts who are reputable in their field, and so forth. We have to learn whom to trust, and this is often a long process during which we will make our fair share of mistakes, but what is the alternative? To become credulous and uncritical?

Trust Is Not Uncritical

Evidence leads you to judgments. It makes you believe certain things, and one of the most sobering truths of critical thinking is that it prepares you to follow the evidence, wherever it leads. Such openness also includes the acknowledgment that the evidence we have *now* might be overturned in the future, either because there is new evidence or because new experiences make us weigh our initial evidence differently. The quest for truth often leads us in directions we do not want to go. This, however, requires that the evidence we follow be *reliable*. The way the evidence was measured must either be from a trustworthy process (e.g., fingerprint analysis) or from a trustworthy source (e.g., a respectable scientific lexicon or person).

It is important to note that *trust* by itself is not uncritical. Human life does not function without trust, and neither does science. We rely on the trustworthy witness in a criminal trial just as we rely on astronomers giving us the correct data about the planets of our universe. We cannot fact-check everything; it is impossible. Yet this does not mean that such trust is uncritical or undiscerning. I have used the *Oxford English Dictionary* many times in my life, and each time I have found it to be reliable, which is why I trust it. I trust my electrician because he has done excellent work in the past and reliably informed me about various problems in my house. Trust is the result of a *prior verification* and thus the opposite of credulity.

Factors that can help me to discern whether a source is reliable are past performance, which is a good indicator for future performance, and some background on the *guiding principles* of my source: Is she engaged in rigorous research and inquiry, and do the people involved have any reason to give me false information?

Following reliable and trustworthy evidence can, however, have unforeseen consequences. Good examples are the biographies of two famous philosophers. For decades, Antony Flew's little but brilliant book *God and Philosophy* (1966) was required reading in practically every seminar on atheism. It was one of the sharpest rejections of faith one could find. For Flew, there was no evidence that could justify belief in God. In the 2000s, however, Flew confessed that new evidence gathered from physics and biology had convinced him that God existed after all.[9] Likewise, Alasdair MacIntyre, a famous Scottish thinker and ardent atheist (and Marxist), changed his mind about the existence of God after a long search for truth and is today a practicing Catholic (and my university colleague).[10]

Distrust and Illiteracy Are the Problems!

Thus far, I have avoided the elephant in the room: What if you cannot trust? After all, trust is built on positive experiences. I trust an author because she has informed me reliably in the past, or I trust a friend because we have shared many personal experiences and she has never betrayed me. Many in today's society cannot or do not want to trust authors or newspapers or the sciences. Instead, people are celebrating doubt and uncertainty about things that are scientifically highly probable (I use this phrase because there are not many things that can be "proven" in the strict sense of the word).

A good example of this is *human-produced climate change*. Almost every specialist agrees on it, but of course you have some outliers who don't. Instead of trusting the wider scientific community, though, many choose to believe the voices at the fringe because they distrust any consensus and expect that a conspiracy always lies behind it. But why?

People usually distrust others because they have had bad experiences. In an America in which salaries have stagnated for decades and in which many people have slid down the social ladder, it is not surprising to find a big crowd that feels disenfranchised. Such people have lost hope because their dreams have been crushed and the promises that had been given to them have never been kept.

The phenomena of universal and unfounded doubt of science (which leads to the denial of climate change) and distrust of medicine (which paved the way for the antivaccine movement) rest largely on a campaign started in the 1960s by a handful of scientists in order *to create such distrust*. Supported by powerful firms, these researchers made a living by becoming the fringe voices of science, convincing the public that scientific consensus *always* warrants suspicion. In this way scapegoats were created: scientists, politicians, and lobbyists spread lies, such as human-made climate change, in order to extort money from the already financially disadvantaged.

Therefore, these researchers reason, you cannot trust scientists, because they are out to get your money and your freedom. Moreover, as Stanley Fish has shown, this campaign also proved very successful because it *flattered* the public into believing it could judge debates between scientists. "Saying 'you be the judge' is always a good rhetorical move, especially when the 'you' being deferred to doesn't know what it's talking about and can be led to any conclusion desired by a master manipulator."[11]

I don't think, however, that this is the entire story! Every couples therapist will, for example, tell you that a main reason for lost trust in a marriage is the lack of a language that both partners understand. Scientists and researchers of all persuasions have, especially in the last few decades, lived an intellectually incestuous life in their ivory towers, writing their articles for a handful of peers but largely failing to communicate their findings to the common people.

Most Americans do not have the ability to follow the subtle, sophisticated debates of these great scholars and thus feel excluded from knowledge that impacts their life this way or another. Many of these also do not understand that scientific knowledge changes and that some things held to be true fifty years ago are no longer considered valid today, while *truth* in their lives does not change so easily.

Too often, however, the researchers themselves shy away from popularizing their findings, and so they leave it to intellectual conmen, who make a quick buck but do not really educate the public. Subdued literacy is thus a real obstacle to good reasoning and critical thinking! Literacy is more than the mere reading of words; it is rather the ability to *comprehend* their meaning and their context.

Every high school teacher will tell you how hard it is nowadays to even choose a printed text for students, because so many students cannot understand relatively easy grammatical structures. A way out of the uncritical and uninformed circle of distrust is *literacy education* and raising literacy standards.[12] At the same time, though, academics have to be educated about how to become effective teachers for the wider public, give up their scientific language for ordinary prose, and thus accept their responsibility for the educational state of the nation.

Overcoming Confirmation Bias

You might object now and say, "That is all well and good, but how do I learn to ask critical questions?" My best advice is to acquaint yourself with the tools and methods of philosophy. Philosophy establishes causes and effects, and it therefore rejects simplistic explanations by demanding justifications for them. It requires that the presuppositions of our arguments, as well as our assumptions, be thoroughly vetted.

Confirmation bias,[13] in which you reinforce your preconceived ideas and "fillet" your evidence accordingly, is therefore the *arch-enemy* of philosophy, because it makes a mockery of the search for truth and wisdom.

Biased reason or *confirmation bias* seems to be based largely on *intuition*. One can see this most clearly in how we make decisions. In psychological experiments, human test subjects usually neglected to seek counterevidence and most often chose spontaneously and thus based on intuition rather than reasoning. Arguments *in favor of* their choices were only invented by the test subjects *after* the choice, while arguments *against* one's choice did not, by and large, even enter their minds. This experiment showed that humans have a strong tendency not to *think of counterarguments* in their decision-making process but to trust their "gut."

By merely relying on intuition, such confirmation bias only uses a fraction of our brain power, and perhaps that's why we are naturally inclined to follow it, but it is *lazy* and never allows us to reach our full potential.

Perhaps worse, such bias leads people into relationships of dependency and makes them easily exploitable. The only way out seems to be *serious critical thinking* in which we face the toughest objections and counterarguments. It is easy to think of ideas we disagree with, but hard to imagine arguing against ideas that are dear to us. Yet this is what made the great philosophers (especially the Scholastics) "great." That's exactly what, for example, Thomas Aquinas did. If you open the *Summa contra Gentiles* or *Summa Theologiae*, you will see that he always chooses to defeat the strongest counterargument first and often makes it even stronger than it actually is.[14]

7

Without Order There Is No Good Reasoning

I was about eleven years old when I lost my bike. At first, I thought it was stolen because it was not in our garage, but after I thought about it, I remembered that I had left it in the church parking lot. Luckily, it was still there when I went to retrieve it the next day. This sort of thing happened to me a lot, and slowly but surely I came to the conclusion that I was more absentminded than other kids my age. I decided that I needed a better way of living my life so that I would stop getting lost in my thoughts and losing things. It was very fortunate for me that, around this time, I had schoolteachers who exposed me to actual philosophy. Beginning in fifth grade Latin we read snippets from Seneca and Cicero, and in ninth grade Greek we studied Plato and Aristotle. The rigor of philosophical thinking challenged me to order my thoughts, too, and to imitate what I had learned. Philosophy saved my life!

A Grid Brings Order

Philosophy provided my mind with *order*, and it gave me a *map for the relationships of things*. *Order* means that more than two things are arranged according to a common relationship (e.g., the books in my office are arranged by topic). Order includes hierarchies as well, where some things have a more exalted place than others. Order is the compass our mind uses to find its bearings because without it our thinking would be aimless, like swimming in an ocean without knowing where land can be found.

While order is the guiding aim, *method* is how we achieve order in our thinking. Method shows us which way to choose on our quest for truth (the Greek word for *method* means "with a way"). To work efficiently, a method has to be *systematic*. It has to outline a process or a body of actions that we follow. These steps have been proven to lead to reliable results. A methodical search will lead to reliable end results, to certainty in knowledge. This is the basic idea of methods, both in the humanities and in the hard sciences.

Such an endeavor differentiates systematic, methodical work from an aimless search or a lucky find—the latter has no clear goal and no prescribed steps, rendering its knowledge shaky and minimal. Having a method is like having a treasure map that describes the dangers and the booby traps along the way and how to avoid them. The more precise you are about your method, the more successful your research will be, because you will be focused and your results will be reliable. Creating and following a method will also enable you to convey your findings to your readers in a clear and structured manner. Communication is more effective if your listener or reader can follow the order of your arguments.[1]

The progress of science hinges largely on the ability of scientists to freely discuss their work and read about each other's work. Yet words and sentences need order; otherwise they are just dots on a piece of paper. The more ordered our sentences are, the higher the chance that we are understood. As a person with ADHD, I can tell you that despite all my efforts, I am still puzzled by those who live with me, and sometimes they think the way my mind works is confusing. Even my spouse of twenty years is sometimes baffled. She once mentioned making something vegetarian for dinner, which made me think of health, so I asked her, "Are health care stocks anti-cyclical?" She looked at me like I had lost my mind, but once I explained to her my way of ordering things, I no longer sounded so crazy.

Explaining your methods is not only helpful for improving your work and arguments, but it can also ease tension and improve your quality of life, because people will better understand *how* you think.

Thinking Coherently Takes Effort

When we present a more complex argument, we have to make sure we present our thinking coherently. We must lay out our arguments clearly. When somebody tells us we don't make any sense, they usually mean that our sentences lack such a form. After all, we didn't talk gibberish, but formed whole sentences, so why did our dialogue partner not understand us?

Such clarity is often called *coherence*, and it describes how sentences or things hang together. When a person does not understand me, she is not able to see what I'm trying to get at because something is blocking it. Most likely I was not able to put things into an order that makes the meaning I want to convey obvious.

Every judgment we give, such as "The tree is green," contains a subject ("tree"), a predicate ("green"), which may also include an object, and a copula ("is"), which connects them. When we have trouble understanding someone, it is often because we do not know what either the subject or the predicate is. That, or we cannot see the relation between sentences or sentence parts, which causes us to reject our dialogue partner's conclusion.

Given the fact that no one is infallible, I tend to think that incoherence often occurs due to our *own* inability to listen properly. Social media seems to have made this incompetence a virtue. Let me give you an example: I have an excellent memory, but my ADHD testing proved to me that while I am extremely attentive to what I find interesting, I have shockingly low retention for what I find boring. So, before I respond to an argument I can't make sense of, I try to ask myself: "Did I really pay attention? Is there something I have overlooked?" Changes in behavior do not happen overnight, and some things change only slowly over time, but from my own experience I can say that setting and keeping rules for my listening and reading helps me to be more generous to others and to myself.

In addition to such exterior coherence, there is also an *inner coherence*: We call a sentence coherent if it makes sense *and is true*—that is, if there is no inner logical contradiction. The claim that $1 + 1 = 3$ cannot be true because it contradicts the laws of logic, and therefore it is incoherent. Yet the sentence "All Wisconsinites like cheese" is coherent and logically possible but ultimately false (my daughter is living proof of that).

So, it is not just the order of the argument but also its *inner logic* that we have to pay attention to. If my claims contradict the laws of logic, they render it impossible for my dialogue partner to "see" the meaning I intend, because the structure has a serious flaw.

My claims do not even have to contain logical contradictions to achieve this unhappy result: it is enough to *neglect* logical possibilities or implications to flaw our argument. When we searched for a new house a year ago, because we were moving to Indiana, I wanted to buy a smaller one than the one we had in Wisconsin. I thought of heating costs, carbon footprint, and of the possibility of being empty nesters in a huge home. I completely neglected the logical consequence that small children grow up to be big children and that teenagers need more space than toddlers. My argument was not built on logic but on partial logic; my reasoning was not coherent because my idea did not mesh well with the reality that we have five kids. It failed the coherency test!

Philosophical thinking guards us from being *rash* with our statements. "All Wisconsinites like cheese" is logically possible but fails the rashness test. All too quickly, we have generalized something before checking possible counterevidence (like my daughter).

Therefore, a sentence has a higher grade of coherence not only if it is logically possible but also if we take into account (a) what it might be like for it to be true and (b) what it might be like for all statements *entailed by it* to be true. Had we stopped and applied the two additional *criteria*, we would have been prevented from making the rash judgment. After all, can we really make sense of (a) the claim that *all* Wisconsinites like cheese and (b) the statement that cheese is a *necessary* food for *all* Wisconsinites (a "truth" entailed by claim *a*)?[2]

I hope this chapter has shown how important order and coherence are, not just for our thinking but also for fruitful communication with other people. If we think about how to communicate more clearly and coherently, it is more likely we will be heard and understood, and hopefully become better listeners as well. Intellectual humility has always been a virtue among the philosophers, and I believe that a society shaped by it would be a more virtuous one too.

8

Ignorance Is Not Bliss

O nce one of my college professors remarked that "philoso-phy helps to answer questions we would not have without philosophy." Wouldn't it be better not to have philosophy at all then? We wouldn't have to bother with any of this! Yet is such blissful ignorance really possible and desirable? I think not, especially if we desire to improve our thinking and empower our mind. An ignorant mind is, after all, always a *weak* mind.

Ignorance as a Moral Weakness

Ignorance as a willful rejection of learning becomes dangerous if it is paired with arrogance. It quickly leads to disregard for others and an inflated view of oneself. People who act in willful ignorance do not check their own prejudices or their courses of action. Such people do not engage in critical thinking and rational behavior, and, of course, they neglect the crucial question, "Do I have a moral obligation to know x?"[1]

Moreover, the person who has the faculties of reasoning can hardly box them up and put them away. But there are also people who are not willfully ignorant but who simply don't care for knowledge. Could it be that they are happier because they never developed the same appetite or learned to reason like I did? I really don't know the answer to that, because I can't speak for them; yet I think that if nature has endowed us with faculties, we should use them, which is not the same as saying we should do everything that is within the reach of these faculties, such as inflicting violence on others.

Psychologists have found that intelligence alone has no independent influence on how satisfied you feel with your life. Nevertheless, reasoning influences underlying factors immensely: people who think critically are less likely to suffer from *anomia*, the failure to remember and name objects or concepts. And if you cannot properly name and identify objects, you lose your orientation. This is not only the experience of dementia patients but also to a diminished degree what happens in our world: the less we *use reason*, the less likely we are to find orientation in our increasingly complex world.[2]

An even more important advantage of the critically thinking person is her ability to grasp reality. If we do not attempt to look at the sources of our information about the world, we will probably be deceived often. Knowing what the real world is, however, is needed for us to find the real good in it and also to identify the dangers and pitfalls.

Better Thinking Can Save Our Failing Society

Reason is a great way to deal with information overload, fake news, and consumer manipulation; it also helps us make sense of societal transformations such as demographic changes or the adoption of new societal values. Reason operates, as we have seen, on the basis of certain laws and rules, and critical thinking instills disciplined thought. Such discipline has been shown to be one of the most important factors for a successful life.

Using education to unlock the power of reason is also a good way to change our hopelessly failing prison system. Being tough on crime has been largely ineffective. If we look at juvenile offenders, for instance, empowering their minds and opening their eyes to the values of education and self-discipline can be life transforming. If we did a better job in schools, we could stop many criminal careers before they even begin. Over half of the children who become juvenile offenders were a year behind their peers by the time they reached the second grade. Future criminal activity often has its roots in elementary school![3]

Finding better ways to integrate critical thinking into our schools, though, does not mean raising a generation of nerds who have no practical skills. Practical knowledge and good reasoning have to go hand in hand. After all, hands-on experience helps you to understand the world more fully. If you try to determine what material is lying on your potter's wheel while wearing a blindfold, you will suddenly feel aspects of the material that you didn't recognize before. If somebody switches the clay for porcelain, you will quickly realize the difference. Suddenly, you become aware of the different textures and densities of the material, all the hidden details and dimensions. The more our mind is in touch with these details, practical *and* intellectual, the more attentive it is to the small things in life, also and especially in our personal relationships. Your life will be the happier for it.[4]

Overcoming Ignorance Drives Innovation

Socrates, the father of Greek philosophy, allegedly remarked once, "All I know is that I know nothing."[5] Philosophy done properly teaches humility and the realization that the more we find out about ourselves and the world, the more we don't know, because for each answer we find myriad other questions. Think of Isaac Newton discovering gravity and explaining why things fall to the ground. Yet he could not figure out *what* this gravity really was and where it came from. His discovery opened up a number of new research questions. Ignorance can be immensely productive because we try to overcome it, but we never fully defeat it.[6] It is like a perennial thorn in our flesh; we pull it out of our toe only to realize we have acquired a new one in our palm.

This way, ignorance drives innovation and especially scientific discoveries. The clue is, however, to *articulate your ignorance* properly. I realize this sounds odd. What I mean is: The better you are able to express what you *do not know*, the better the questions you are trying to answer will be, and consequently also the results. Yes, there is an art to asking the right questions, and it is hard work. I sometimes push my students in the classroom when they tell me, after I ask them a question, "I don't know." "Well, explain to me *what* you don't know!" They look puzzled and stutter around a bit, but if you help them articulate their ignorance, you can often see the light bulb go on, and they are able to answer the question by themselves.

By carefully *describing what we do not know*, we define an area of research. We identify the borders between knowledge and ignorance, and by doing so, we find out more about the details of what we are looking for. Daniel DeNicola calls this practice "ignorance mapping."[7] By the time the question is formulated, it will be focused enough that it can guide your research and lead to good results. In fact, I have found that ignorance mapping *empowers* you to search in the right direction and can get you out of the trenches. For me, it often jump-started a project that had stalled for a long time.

At the beginning of this chapter, I mentioned in passing that sometimes we have a *moral obligation* to know. A lawyer is professionally obliged to know the law, my electrician the handling of wires, and school children (and college students?) are obliged to learn. Yet do we all have a duty to overcome ignorance?

Citizens of a society have certain rights and duties defined by law, but they are also bound by universal moral obligations, such as treating others respectfully. If reason is such a powerful tool for creating flourishing lives and institutions, would we not also be obliged to use it to fight ignorance that endangers lives and well-being?

When I lived in Germany, we had a terrible outbreak of measles because anti-vaxxers had successfully convinced many parents that it would be safer and more natural not to vaccinate their kids. The outbreak cost a number of lives, including some new-born babies, and it endangered pregnant women and their unborn babies—all of which could have been prevented.

I would argue that as a citizen, I have the responsibility to *evaluate* claims that could endanger the lives of my children—or the life of any person, for that matter. I have a responsibility to overcome my ignorance and not give in to the first conspiracy theory I encounter.

Of course, should my rational faculties be impeded, my responsibility might be diminished. I can't be expected to study everything that comes my way, but for matters such as the example above, it is important to make a *serious effort* to inform myself and determine whether a claim is based on flawed methodologies. The tools of philosophical thought, especially critical thinking, can and should be applied to see which "facts" are truly facts and which are not.

9

Real Thinking Sets You Free

Thornton Wilder once remarked, "The more decisions that you are forced to make alone, the more you are aware of your freedom to choose."[1] Sometimes such decisions can be painful, especially if we have no one to confide in, and sometimes they are terrifying because it becomes obvious to us that our life will never be the same after we make them. Yet in order to make *good decisions*, we *have to* think and know. Freedom is only worth half as much if we don't have the knowledge to use it well.

Remember that the original name for a general education was "liberal arts." The liberal arts were designed to set people free from only focusing on their survival in order to discover other important things about life, such as truth, beauty, goodness, and virtue, but also vice and evil. Liberal arts free us from the prison of ourselves and our own loneliness because they expose us to artists, poets, and writers, to great ideas and stories. They show us what it means to be part of the human family and to find a place in it. Ultimately, they make us aware of what our freedom enables us to do and to achieve.

Freedom, however, is often undermined in our world, sometimes directly but most often in secret. It usually starts in middle or high school, when students are told their minds and souls are merely a series of "brain events."

The implication is clear: there is *no universal morality*, *no universal rationality*, only gene-driven, selfish people. In such a worldview, it makes no sense to stress "freedom of choice" as often happens, because it is incompatible with a determinism that *denies* free will. Don't get me wrong, I love science, but this kind of biology is *bad* science because it teaches a blunt, contradictory naturalism.

Likewise, when Silicon Valley heroes tell us that our brains are supercomputers, they do not imply that humanity is great but rather that there are no such things as *valuable individuality* and freedom. Brains are interchangeable, like software, and consequently, human bodies become unimportant puppets you can fool around with in manifold ways.

This chapter tries to unearth consequences such as these because determinism and naturalism are worldviews that pose a serious danger to our democracy and our human rights.

Freedom and Reason Need Each Other

A number of scientists and philosophers tell us we are not free and that we are fully determined by our genes. They claim that the freedom we experience is an illusion. This theory is called *determinism*. According to determinism, large areas of our lives, those in which we painfully or joyfully make important choices, are predetermined by forces beyond our control. Our present and past decisions are not our own, and as a consequence, neither are our future choices. Our mind is not in the driver's seat but strapped to a booster chair in the back; there is no freedom and therefore no intentional choice or creativity.

Without freedom, there are no such things as reason and rationality but only the force of nature. Reason entails that we choose arguments freely because we have discovered something true or false about them, but if you eliminate freedom from it, nothing worthwhile remains. To be clear, I am not denying that some factors (e.g., upbringing, temperament) *can diminish* or *influence* our freedom, but they *do not eradicate* it. Only in very rare circumstances is our freedom completely diminished (e.g., when we are under the influence of drugs). Identifying such influences and debating them (e.g., in the context of judicial reform) does not mean defending determinism. Every philosopher knows that there is no such thing as perfect freedom among human beings because we all have limitations. Having a vigorous understanding of freedom does not mean denying its limitations, but it does entail rejecting the determinist view that freedom is an illusion.

A denial of freedom is a serious attack on human morality and reason, because reason and freedom are *mutually* dependent. Neither can exist without the other. Whenever I accept a rational argument, I am freely choosing to do so because I have understood it, and it was intelligible to me. In a deterministic world, I cannot trust reason, because I *cannot* freely choose an option. Whatever the result of my decision, I was never free to choose it.

I live in a world in which the loudest voice wins—the one that intimidates me the most by activating my genetic defense mechanisms. I live in a world in which I cannot trust my own insights because they are not mine and are produced by forces outside my control. I live in a world in which I cannot trust anybody because everybody is driven by their genes, just like I am.

The scenario of such a deterministic world is one in which hatred becomes a standard human expression, for which people no longer apologize: hatred becomes an accepted reaction to certain things. Since in my deterministic worldview I have eliminated freedom and reason, I don't even have to try to subject my emotions to reason. I don't need to calm my hatred because it is "natural." After all, my reactions are preprogrammed. Do you want to live in such a world?

If we do not recover a culture in which we *trust reason*, there is no reason at all. The world is then just ruled by things we cannot choose to inquire about, because we are driven by other forces.

Yet if there is no freedom, then our minds cannot freely accept some arguments while rejecting others. Consequently, there would be no *rational freedom*, no rationality. Wrestling with ideas or trying to convince others would be a waste of time. Whoever is stronger has the right to dominate others; human rights can be changed accordingly.

Therefore, if you are not free to choose a political worldview, there is no reason why a deterministic society should or would allow *freedom of speech*. I shudder when I think of such a world and society, and as a German I cannot help but connect it to what my country went through in the twentieth century. Both Nazism and Communism embraced a determinist worldview in which "fate" was the overarching principle. Individual lives did not count for very much. Both of these regimes suppressed free discourse and rationality, and both resulted in mass murder. Denying freedom of expression fits into these and other deterministic worldviews because freedom has no value for them.[2]

Is My Experience of Freedom Reliable?

Is freedom something we experience? I would say yes. I am free to write this page or not. I could have decided not to write a chapter on freedom too.

In some situations in our life it can happen that we feel *compelled* to make a decision and perhaps doubt that we are free. Yet feeling pressure to make a decision does not mean that there is no freedom but rather that it is so deeply ingrained in our existence that we recognize forces trying to influence us. After all, proper decision making depends on freedom. Humans are *forced to be free*—that is the irony of our existence.

You still might not be convinced, and you might ask for more proof. However, you should consider that human freedom is a commonly held assumption, and because it is the basis for our judicial system, our electoral system, and so on, the person denying it has the *burden of proof*. Arguing in favor of human freedom, however, does not mean that nothing can influence or in some cases even diminish our freedom. In fact, our genes and our upbringing heavily *influence* our moral character.

Nevertheless, the foundation of all ethics is that there exists a "*should*, which is not a *must*, which presupposes an active free will."[3] In a deterministic world, there are no *shoulds* because there is no "being able to do *x* freely." The denial of free will leads to the denial of human beings being able to freely make choices, and therefore to the eradication of all moral responsibility.

How can I attribute the actions I have committed to myself if I deny my own part in choosing them? Is there even something like "humanity" left in a world that is fully determined? After all, the concept of "will," which so many boast about, doesn't make sense in a world without free will. Since will is the power of decision making, which is based on freedom, there can be no "will" but merely the rule of brutal force by instinct and emotion.

Some people forget that in a deterministic world, they would also have to say farewell to love as the free giving of oneself to another, friendship, and so much more . . . to everything that presupposes deliberate choice and reason.

Save Your Freedom by Thinking

One of my favorite things to do online is watching philosophical debates. Whenever I tune in to disputes between scientists and philosophers about free will, I am puzzled: The scientist often vehemently argues against free will but lacks any self-awareness with regard to his position. He cannot see the contradiction in trying to convince others to accept his argument, which is only possible through free will, while at the same time denying the existence of free will. Is there a better example of what philosophers call *performative contradiction*?

By having learned how to reason well, you will be able not only to see obvious contradictions but also to discover deeper flaws in someone's argument. Let's consider the scientist from our debate for a moment.

If the scientist denies free will, he also either ignores or forgets that the *most basic principle of scientific experimentation* in a lab is that the variable conditions for such an experiment are *freely chosen* by the person running it. Therefore, a scientist denying free will *denies the foundations of his own science*, cutting off the branch he is sitting on.

And let's push our reasoning further and apply it to this scientist being on a TV show: Why would he even engage in an argument to convince someone that free will does not exist, if according to him there is no free decision making? If determinism were true, such a scientist would (if he were true to his principles) have to *manipulate* us but *not reason* with us. After all, manipulation is licit because you do not violate anyone's freedom, which does not exist.[4]

I wonder why so few people see this and still debate determinism or celebrate it as a masterful new idea. No, determinism is antihuman and by definition unintelligent, because it rejects rationality.

Freedom Is More Than Choice

If you listen to debates between politicians, you could get the impression that freedom is merely the "freedom to choose." Certainly, that is an important part of it, but it is not the most important aspect of freedom. Only in the last few hundred years has this been touted as the core of freedom, but over the last decades philosophers have realized that ancient thinkers, such as Aristotle or the medieval genius Aquinas, had some better things to say about freedom than John Locke did.

Classical philosophy, until the beginning of modernity, understood that the choices you make mold you into a certain kind of person. Freedom did not mean belonging to oneself and one's "choices" but rather belonging to the Good. Before we have a relationship to family and society, we have one to the Good.

For Aquinas we participate in the Good because we exist. Reason as the basis for choice is for the Greek philosopher Plato a power that comes about in the soul by the presence of the Good in our soul. Consequently, choice is only possible because of the Good.[5] To reduce freedom to mere choice is a bit like reducing wine to a thirst-relieving libation: it is made primarily for a different purpose, and using it this way abuses the very essence of wine.

Likewise, for Aristotle or Aquinas, it was not only important *that* you have a choice (which is what most modern philosophers understand by freedom) but especially *what* you choose. Only choosing the Good makes you free, while choosing evil enslaves you and drags you down to vice.

The more I freely choose to act in a good and virtuous manner, the freer my actions will be. When I commit myself fully and freely in marriage, for example, and bind myself to a spouse, I am committing a valuable act of freedom with which I eliminate future freedom of choice (for another partner—this is the foundation of fidelity).

Such a free decision for a good (which could be a certain lifestyle too) is *essentially symbolic*. It signifies that I am joining myself to a certain good. Such a symbolic action, with which I indicate the future elimination of some of my choices, must also be of higher value than nonsymbolic choices. Raising my left arm "is far less free than the pronouncing of the marriage vow, since there is very little determination of the self," because I do not let a good *influence* (not determine!) me.[6]

Once you realize that not all choices are cut from the same cloth, you will probably laugh when you read example stories for free choice in ethics textbooks, which do not even consider such a difference. Yet it all boils down to the question of whether you believe that a good life is shaped by a freedom that is influenced by real goods, or whether you believe freedom is only about human actions that are independent of any good.

Another problem with the sole emphasis on choice is that it disconnects us from reality. The classical idea of free will accepts that there are goods that are outside of myself and worth pursuing, even if that means limiting my own freedom.

Yet the modern, Lockean approach rejects this idea. It is only the power of choice in the "I," who chooses, that counts. The goods that I choose are irrelevant and only play the role of "options" that I can grasp or reject. For Locke as for most of his contemporaries, freedom is merely about the power to choose completely *unrelated* to goods. For them it is important that I have the choice to either live or commit suicide, but not whether being alive is a good we should not give up.

Thus in the modern, Lockean society, choices are no longer determined by their inherent goodness but merely by the power of choosing that is invested in a person. Choice is then no longer about reality and real goods but about my *preferences* and my *construction* of the world.

Ultimately, this mindset leads to the vice of pride because it does not acknowledge the need to get in touch with things, and instead dismisses them. It is also the mindset of moral monstrousness because it disentangles choice from good and is in principle able to justify *any* evil under the sun. Lastly, it is the worldview of *decayed reason*, as rational faculties are no longer used to encounter the real but just the power of human choice.

I have no doubt that if one analyzed the current environmental crisis, the decay of human rights, and more, at the very root we would find the Lockean destruction of freedom. Compare this dire philosophy to the classical standpoint that we achieve in the free binding of one's freedom *the* most valuable act of free will itself! The philosophies of Plato, Aristotle, Aquinas, and others defend the idea that the goods a human person chooses determine the goodness of the person's life. Is there a good I would give my freedom up for? Perhaps for the love of a spouse, the pursuit of meaning in life, profound friendships, or God?

The Pinnacle of Freedom Is Forgiveness

To forgive someone who has deliberately hurt us or our loved ones must be among the hardest things a person can do. Moreover, forgiveness goes against our natural instincts. It is easy to feel hatred, anger, resentment, and the desire for revenge after suffering an injustice. Even if we do not show it, these feelings often remain with us, possibly because they are tied to a natural self-defense instinct. The philosophical school of the German Max Scheler encouraged people to observe such feelings carefully because they give us clues of how to become more ethical human beings.

When do you feel deeply hurt by someone and react with hatred? If my friend teases me for my absentmindedness, I do not feel such hurt—but if someone outside my circle of friends publicly points it out and tries to embarrass me, I might. But why? Wasn't it the same information, just communicated differently? Yes, it was, but the actions were different: my friend has my well-being in mind and thus has good intentions, while the other wants to humiliate me and perhaps attack my livelihood.

From my own perspective, I know my friend's good intentions and can tell him to stop if I think he is going too far, but this is not the case in the other example. The person seems like he is trying to hurt me, and simply asking him to stop may not do the trick. This is quite an important discovery because it shows us that to a large extent, *our reaction* determines whether we will be overpowered by hatred. We react with outrage when we feel

devalued and dehumanized. Rage and feelings of revenge overpower us because they address our need for defending our value,
especially in moments when we cannot defend ourselves properly;
we think we must do something. Think of social media: somebody
attacks you, and while you can answer with a post of defense, it
is not a real-life, real-time defense, and thus you will feel a desire
for revenge because you cannot shield yourself against the attack.

When we carefully observe such rage, we will find that it is
almost always disproportional and never satisfying. The attacker
will likewise feel resentment and counter, and we enter a vicious
circle that drains our mental health and quality of life. We get
sucked down into the darkness of evil.

Yet reason empowers us to break out of this vicious cycle in a
number of ways. It enables us to identify unjustified attacks so
that we do not even engage in a defense. Reason, however, also
empowers us to face our own wrongdoing and overcome feelings
of guilt by repenting. By honestly confronting our bad actions,
doing penance (in whatever way), and asking for forgiveness, we
save the past *and* gain a future.[7]

Asking for forgiveness and the act of forgiving are both actions
of freedom and autonomy. By doing penance and by forgiving
others we state that we are not and will not be driven by desires
and emotions and that we abandon the vicious cycles of guilt and
revenge. A person who is able to do both, however, knows that
her dignity is *never* wiped out by a bad action and that she does
not receive her value from the outside but from within. The spirit
of forgiveness liberates us from "the spirit of self-enslavement to
an endless chain of destructive violence," says a contemporary
German philosopher.[8]

This is easily said but difficult to achieve because it also entails
the acknowledgment of not being blameless, perhaps not in the
instance in which we were hurt, but in many others in which we
hurt others. We do not often ask for forgiveness, because we fear
being humiliated. Is there no way to avoid such a dilemma?

The philosopher Klaus-Michael Kodalle, who wrestled his whole life with the riddle of forgiveness, stated that acknowledgment of one's own evils is much easier when forgiveness is offered *beforehand*. This is an interesting observation because it enables one also to read the "our Father" prayer philosophically. It states: "*And forgive us our trespasses as we forgive those who trespass against us.*" True forgiveness hinges on the ready availability to forgive on both sides and is never just a singular instance. It is a culture of life, which we decide to freely embrace. Admitting to ourselves that we commit evil and need forgiveness enables us not only to break free from the vicious cycles of revenge and hatred but also to forgive others.

Philosophy helps to discover the freedom to forgive and to receive such forgiveness.

10

Thinking Happens in a Soul, Not a Computer

At the beginning of the book, we discussed nonmaterial things such as laws, the experience of ourselves, and our thoughts. Many philosophers try to explain these via *naturalism*, which essentially means that everything we encounter can be explained by the natural sciences, even if we do not fully understand everything yet.

Naturalism is based on one major premise or foundation—namely, that the world is like a closed box, *and* all the answers we seek can be found within it, never outside of it. Since this is an "all-" sentence, a proposition explaining everything, it is a claim that can be neither proven nor falsified by empirical sciences, because it is a *metaphysical* claim.

As such, it illustrates a typical *overreach* of the sciences into philosophy. This becomes obvious when we look closer at what naturalism has to say about the human person. In a naturalist world, in which only the empirically verifiable exists, there is no real understanding for conscious "animals" like human beings and their individual views of themselves and the world (the first-person perspective). The naturalist description "person x feels pain" will never be equivalent to the first-person perspective of *my* pain.

Moreover, according to the second guiding maxim of naturalism, science can never have any recourse to, or even ask for, the *final causes* of things, their ends. The search for such ends is called *teleology*, a word that comes from the Greek word for "end" (*telos*). For example, the scientist cannot ask for the final cause of this universe—that is, for what purpose it exists. The moment one asks such a question, one leaves behind what the sciences can buttress and enters the field of metaphysics/philosophy. Yet if confronted with human actions, a naturalist suddenly *has* to accept teleological explanations. After all, we constantly judge human actions according to ends. Let us suppose a researcher sabotages one of his supervisor's experiments. Obviously, he will be asked for his motives, for the ends and purposes of his actions. Humans always have goals and ends.[1] And as I pointed out above, although the naturalist has to accept this reality, he does not have the means to adequately deal with it.

The depth of the human person remains unreachable for him because of the restraints of his approach. He stays on the surface of the third-person description. I spent so much time with this because it is crucial to understand it: Naturalism, which attempts to explain the human experience, fails miserably to grasp this mystery. And if it tries to do so, it overreaches into an area where the sciences are incompetent—namely, philosophy. The debate about our brains as computers, which we'll discuss more fully below, shows this beautifully.

Don't Get Robbed of Your First-Person Experience

A naturalist would probably try to convince us that "laws" are not immaterial things, as we saw in chapter 3, but merely words we create to put order into our thinking. She would say, "All such alleged immaterial phenomena can be explained by natural causes within the world of science." But wait a second! Do you see what the naturalist just did? She simply claimed that all immaterial things can be *reduced* to material explanations. Yet how can immaterial things, such as thoughts and laws, be reduced to mere physicality?

We can certainly find out what happens in the brain if I think of the concept "law," but that does not help us understand why "I" understand it. Or take the example of pain and joy: "I" experience joy seeing my children laughing, and "I" experience pain in my knee. This is totally different from an observer's perspective. The observer or third-person perspective[2] of the scientist is *not identical* with my first-person perspective: "Each subject sees himself as *the one and only subject* of the experience he is having."[3]

The scientist can say that this or that area of your brain is active when you experience joy, but the joy is experienced *uniquely by you*! We have therefore established that there are two fundamentally different perspectives: the naturalist claims our *brain* constructs images, ideas, and feelings, but your experience tells you that *you* see and experience a real thing. If it were true that the brain could create the world outside our bodies, then our knowledge of the brain would also be a construct and an image of an image, which leads us into a loop that never ends. If we accept this theory, we have *no access to reality* at all!

Rather than getting fooled by such cheap naturalism, I think it is much more rational to assume that *we* really experience *the world* because we do not see images but *things*, such as houses, tables, and books.[4]

To sum it up, naturalism attempts to give a *full* description and explanation of the world with the help of the sciences. However, there is no such thing as an objective perspective from which an outsider can describe what goes on inside of me. She can see what areas of my brain are active, whether I shiver and whether I smile, but the pain and joy are mine only. There is an unsurpassable chasm between an outside description of you and your privileged access to yourself.[5] Due to this gap, it seems certain that the sciences (third-person perspective) cannot describe everything and that therefore naturalism cannot be a universal theory of the world.

The second problem an alert thinker easily discovers—and it is closely related to what we just said—is this: How does the naturalist get from statements about my physical body, such as "brain region x is active," to statements about my *mind*, which is something *immaterial*? You cannot get from the brain event "neurons five through ten firing" to the idea of *me* thinking about spring without introducing some kind of *bridge* between material and immaterial things and explaining how they are related.

It is the same type of problem we saw in the previous paragraphs— namely, how you get from a third-person perspective to a first-person perspective—because, unlike a brain event such as "neuron five is active," first-person mental states, such as "I feel uncomfortable when you do that," *cannot* be predicted with absolute certainty.

This explanatory gap between physical brain events and immaterial mind experiences is often elegantly ignored by defenders of naturalism because it exposes how flawed their worldview actually is.[6]

Your Brain Is Not a Computer

Since the above concepts are among the hardest to grasp, it is worth staying with them a bit longer. Perhaps you have never met someone who defended determinism or naturalism as I explained it above. However, I bet you have heard someone say at least once that your brain is like a computer, whether on TV or in a conversation. Such a statement entails naturalism because it denies that there is a mind behind the brain processes. The image of our brain as a computer also creates the false impression that our memories, our identity, and our desires are somehow stored, like on a hard drive, in binary code.

Let's assume for a second that our brain was a computer. If it were, then we could just open it up and see its hardware and operating software. Instead of ones and zeros, we would find your memories, favorite songs, and ideas neatly stored somewhere. Yet has anyone ever found the secret codes the brain uses to save information? Not even close! The comparison of our brain with a computer is not even remotely adequate.

Every computer comes with software, and artificial intelligence "learns" by encountering objects through its software. Our brain, however, is much, much different. As Robert Epstein writes, "Here is what we are not born with: information, data, rules, software, knowledge, lexicons, representations, algorithms, programs, models, memories, images, processors, subroutines, encoders, decoders, symbols, or buffers—design elements that allow digital computers to behave somewhat intelligently. Not only are we not born with such things, we also don't develop them—ever."[7] While computers such as AI retrieve, manipulate, and process information, we really don't do any of those things. That's why we should avoid describing human understanding with computer images such as "processing information." If we do, we have already fallen into the trap of comparing our brains with a computer.

While the computer cannot encounter "world" and "football" but only computerized codes for these things consisting of ones and zeros, we perceive *reality as it is* and do not require a binary code (symbols) in order to do it. Despite this, the metaphor of the brain as a supercomputer has become the standard image used to describe our mental faculties, and in this, naturalism has been very successful. It is problematic, though, because it slowly erodes, as we explained above, trust in reason and freedom.

The rhetoric of comparing brains to computers begins with the reasonable premise that all computers are behaving "intelligently." The second premise is that all computers are information processors, and from that, naturalists conclude that (against all logic!)[8] all beings that behave *intelligently are information processors.* Once you put it like this, you can see the flaws in the argument yourself.

Let's try a little experiment. Get a piece of paper and draw from memory one side of a dollar bill. Perhaps you remembered some of the characteristics, such as George Washington's face, but did you remember which direction he is looking? How often are the words *one* and *Federal Reserve* printed on it, where are the numbers on the note located, and where is the signature of the chair of the Federal Reserve placed? Now take a dollar bill out of your wallet and complete or correct your picture. If your brain was just a computer, why couldn't it retrieve all of the information you missed? Isn't the information for the dollar bill stored in a code somewhere in our brain? No, because human knowledge of the world is holistic; it is about whole things, about reality as such, and not about saving data on a hard drive.

Brain researchers will never find the image of the dollar bill in our brain because it was never stored in our neurons. Instead, our mind possesses an intelligible form of the bill that allows us to visualize it and redraw it. This is not what a computer does!

I am spending so much time on this because I believe comparing our brains to computers has horrible repercussions. If we are reduced to computers, then our identities are in our software, and we can do whatever we wish to our own bodies. The software, however, doesn't have to have a relationship to reality. It can be whatever we want it to be.

This leads first of all to a denigration of the human body. It becomes a mere vessel for the software, which could be discarded, mutilated, or interchanged with someone else's body. In this worldview the body is no longer inherently linked with my mind, and it no longer makes a unity of "me" existing in soul and body but is reduced to a living corpse. Such a crude dualism, however, leads to seeing hurt done to other bodies as equally unproblematic as hurt done to my body.

I cannot see how such a mindset prepares us in any way to respect others and accept that all human beings have inalienable rights. Instead, such thinking leads to what is called *transhumanism*, to the idea that mechanics and computers should be merged with the human body to perfect it.

The goal some transhumanists have is to leave the restrictions of a regular human body behind so that they can someday enjoy eternal life by having their memories "downloaded" to new host bodies or a supercomputer. What hides under the pretext of "perfection of mankind" is in reality *unrestricted selfishness*. Such a person does not want to deal with mortality but wants to enjoy pleasures endlessly. Yet if transhumanists think they can cheat death, they are mistaken. By kicking this can down the road, they hope to never have to answer it because they do not know how. Yet having their immortality on a hard drive or in new bodies is not a desirable immortality because it is intrinsically linked to suffering and to the possibility of death too. After all, somebody could push the reset button on your new body and "you" are gone. This idea of eternity only prolongs desires and fails to fulfill them. It keeps dangling the carrot in front of us but never allows us to eat it. It is not truly eternal life but *counterfeit*. The atheist philosopher Friedrich Nietzsche wisely stated that the endless repetition of the same, never-ending cycle of such a prison of immortality would be a tragic fate that only a superhuman could endure.

These transhumanists overlook that there is no "consciousness software" in our brain that we could download—no brain researcher was ever able to find storage units or identify images or expressions such as Beethoven's Symphony no. 5 in the brain. The brain encounters the world not through mediated binary codes, like even the smartest artificial intelligence does, but directly through the mind.

However, the software comparison has another problem, because each brain is unique due to our DNA. Each one of us reacts differently to the same piece of music or art or food. I love Beethoven while my wife prefers Brahms, and our children cannot stand orchestral music. Our brain structure grows and develops over a lifetime, which is what enables us to *feel differently*.

Transhumanism destroys the idea that humans are individuals who have dignity and reduces them to *machines*. It denies that there are unique experiences that you can't download, such as "the joy of hearing Beethoven," because each of us experiences it differently. Even if we could copy the pattern of billions of neurons, outside of you they are meaningless connections.[9]

This, however, does not mean that our brain is not somehow involved in what and how we think—it would be silly to say that. Even for the most basic tasks we perform, many areas of the brain can be identified as *active*. I hope I have nevertheless shown that naturalism does not work and that the sciences do not explain everything. Moreover, I hope you now see how erroneous it is to compare our brain to a computer, because it is part of a living organism with an immaterial mind. The computer doesn't encounter reality but encounters codes and symbols. Your mind, on the other hand, encounters real things.

Muddy thinking often blurs these important distinctions. It's a bit like comparing solar energy with petroleum-based energy and then concluding that the two are the same because they both power machines. As silly as it sounds, that's the analogous kind of conclusion that leads people to think that our brains are computers. Perhaps you now see why sound reasoning is more important than ever. Not only does it bring us in contact with the most mystifying things in life, but it also challenges us to *clearly* acknowledge differences, even if doing so makes our world more complicated.

Immaterial Matter and the Soul

We saw that the existence of nonmaterial things, like our mind, puzzles us. Many philosophers have believed that the mind of a person could prove the existence of an immortal soul—or something that is not made up of material elements and even survives our physical death. In the nineteenth century, however, natural scientists began to think that the existence of the soul was a fairy tale, but all they had discovered were physical *influences* on our mind such as hormones, sensations, and so on. They no longer believed that there was something immaterial involved in our mental states. For them, the soul was just *matter*, mere brain events.

Although such naturalism still exists and is easily refuted, many philosophers today argue that without mind there cannot be any matter at all and that ultimately, there is mind everywhere in the universe. Moreover, these philosophers remind us that even after decades of groundbreaking research on atoms, neutrons, electrons, and the like, we still have *no idea what this thing we call "matter" really is*. Are atoms and electrons waves or particles or fields? We don't know—perhaps they are all of the above!

Some philosophers of nature have therefore returned to an older view that matter is not just spatial extension. They realized that when physicists speak of mass, they are describing the *relations* between things. But what are the entities that are in relation to each other?

A relationship presupposes that there are *at least* two substances in question. Only because there is a concrete thing A and a concrete thing B can there be a relationship "AB." Without the two carrier substances A and B, there could be no relation between the two. Consequently, if mass is defined by physicists as something that has a relation to energy, velocity, and so on, such a sentence does not tell us *what mass is*, because it only talks about the relationships of mass. The question of what lies underneath the relationship between velocity and mass—namely, what the *carrier substances* of this relationship are—is totally avoided. Most physicists will probably frown at this question or be utterly confused by it, because "physics describes the outside of matter, but not its inner nature," as my teacher in metaphysics used to say.[10]

Despite all our physical knowledge of the universe, we still do not understand fully what matter is, but I think that the solution to the riddle of matter is connected to the riddle that the naturalist denies: the existence of an immaterial mind or soul.

Can Matter Produce Mind?

When we try to explain things, we look for causes, and when we understand them, we find out what their effects are. Yet cause and effect have to be on the same level in order to be related to each other. The philosopher would say they have to be in the same "order of being."

For example, when I look for the cause of my glasses not being on my desk, I could assume that a ghost stole them. Of course that's ridiculous, but bear with me for a moment. Ghosts are in a different category of being, because (if ghosts existed) they are spiritual beings, but the disappearance of my glasses is an empirically verifiable effect. Consequently, I should look for a cause that lies on the same *ontological* level (*ontological* is a fancy word for "being"). Likewise, a human being cannot generate an apple by sheer force of will. The apple is material; our will alone is a mental state. The efficient cause that produces the apple is the apple tree. If we now apply this insight—that cause and effect have to be on the same level of being—to the problem of the mind, we will realize that the naturalist runs into a profound problem.

If the principle we referred to is reliable, then it seems highly unlikely that something *without* a mind (or consciousness), such as the elements of the universe, could produce something like a *mind*. After all, the two belong to two different categories of being. One is part of the *physical* world, the other (like our thoughts) is not. In order to solve this problem, some philosophers have simply claimed that the mind "emerges" from matter. In other words, since there is only matter, it must have somehow produced what we call mind. Now, as fascinating as that sounds, this is an unconvincing argument because this theory doesn't explain *how* the mind emerges or why, just that it somehow does, without any sort of explanation or concept that would *bridge* the material and spiritual world. Instead of putting our head in the sand, we should instead face the inevitable: our minds are made of a different substance than the material world.

If mind can only be produced by mind, then what minds are we talking about? If the world is a web of relationships (mass, velocity, light), what allows these relationships to exist? After all, they exist due to the characteristics of something "underneath." Relationships are always based on real things and must therefore have some kind of carrier "substance." Yet what kind of substance are we talking about? Moreover, since the ultimate laws of the world are indeterminist (that is, they give us only probabilities, not necessities), freedom seems to be woven into the pattern of the universe, but of course freedom needs a carrier substance too.

The puzzle of what the carrier substances could be is the theme of fascinating debates in contemporary philosophy. The theory I find the most interesting is a form of *panpsychism*. While classical panpsychism states that all matter *is* really mind, this newer view argues that all matter is the *expression* of mind. Matter and mind belong together, and this view refutes both monism (only matter exists) and dualism (matter and mind are totally different). For believers in God, this idea has the advantage of suggesting that God can work through the mind-parts of everything that exists, and that God gives those mind-parts freedom to organize themselves. He would be present in and to everything that exists through his mind and their minds. Material things, on the other hand, are expressions of these minds and thus do not exist in a separate sphere. As far-fetched as this theory might sound at first, a number of leading physicists, neurologists, and philosophers believe that it is the most elegant explanation for our riddle.[11]

Personal Identity and Soul

Although in the nineteenth and early twentieth centuries it was fashionable to deny the existence of a soul, it should be clear by now that there are good reasons to argue in favor of its existence. The most important argument for the existence of a soul is probably the experience of personal identity over time. Despite the change in the cells of our bodies, we experience ourselves as the same person. What guarantees such continuity? It must be something underlying the bodily elements—a *substance* that we cannot empirically identify, even if it is somehow tied to our brain. (If our brain is damaged, curiously, our personality *can* change!)

Nevertheless, as I said before, brain and personal identity are not the same. We can make a simple thought experiment: If body parts and personal identity were completely identical, we would be able to say what happens to personal identity if we just knew what happens to the parts of the body. That, however, is not so. I might lose a leg in a car accident, but this information will not let you draw any conclusions about my personality.

When I sense the soft morning breeze through my opened window, my brain reacts to bodily influences. What happens in the brain is called brain events—the interactions of millions of neurons. Yet the brain events and the sensation (of experiencing the breeze) are not the same; they are certainly linked, but they are not identical.

I have already mentioned that sound reasoning deals with distinctions, fine separations, without ripping things apart. Such thinking prevents us from too quickly seeing things as identical and thus committing a serious error in our judgment. This is one of the best examples for the application of this thought: Why would some people assume that brain events and my sensation are identical? Well, because they happen at the same time and in the same body. This sounds reasonable at first, but the moment you dig deeper and ask what kind of properties brain events have and what kind of characteristics sensations have, you will stumble.

Brain events have physical properties: neurons lighting up and giving impulses. How can this be identical to the sensory property of me feeling a breeze? You see—it's not as easy as one might think, neither for the person who claims both are the same nor for the person who claims they are different. Both have to develop a theory of identity that answers such questions.

The question of the soul becomes most important for the riddle of life after death. Most religions teach it, but is it rational to believe in it? If there is indeed this immaterial substance that guarantees continuity throughout our life, why could it not survive the death of our body and brain? Could we not exist in a disembodied state?

Nothing seems to suggest that it is necessary for the soul-substance to have a body. Nevertheless, Thomas Aquinas believed that such a disembodied soul would—because the soul would have previously received all knowledge through the senses—yearn for a new body. Until it was reunited with a new body, the soul would be only a shadow of its former self. Aquinas was, of course, a Christian, and with this argument he made sure to avoid any crude dualism, which would claim we are only souls imprisoned in imperfect bodies. Instead, he made an argument that made the Christian doctrine of the resurrection of the body intelligible.[12]

Yet if there is to be any immortality, a principle of continuity that preserves personal identity, a soul is necessary. How else could we be sure that the person who died is the same in heaven? You might say that a memory transfer could guarantee that, and if God exists, he could simply "upload" those memories to his "cloud." I think, however, that there is a problem here: we are more than our memories. The carrier of the memories is just as important as the memory itself, if it should be "us." Thus, the immaterial soul seems to be a requirement for a postmortem existence.[13]

11

Majority Rules Don't "Make" Truth

Yesterday, I saw a hawk circling above our garden. This statement has a certain truth value; either there was a hawk in
the sky and I saw it, or not. This sounds simple enough,
right? Let's look at some scientific statements (in philosophy we
call them propositions) such as, "The earth orbits the sun." The
truth of the sentence is about the earth and thus about a material,
temporal, changeable thing. It fits the facts or it doesn't. Philosophical propositions, as well as those from the humanities, such
as history, belong to a different category. They are not based on
empirical evidence, such as observation and measuring, but rather
on insight or intuition.

It is important to remember that every thought we have transcends us because the object we are thinking about—let's say the
table I am sitting at ("This table is round")—is not really in me,
but it is also not entirely outside of me either because I am thinking of it in my head. So, what is it? There is a representation of
this table in my mind. So, what could make the sentence "This
table is round" true?

It is true only if the sentence (the representation of the table in
my mind) and its intended content (the table outside my mind) are
participating in the same meaning. After all, they can't be identical

because the table can't be in my head. If there is an *equivalence* between the sentence and the real object, then there must be a third, higher category in which both things participate.[1] (If there is no equivalence, then either we would not understand the sentence or we would immediately recognize its falsity.) Meaning, therefore, goes beyond the media in which it is expressed (either in sentences or in the real world), or as the philosopher would say, it *transcends* (goes beyond) its media.[2]

Therefore, it does not make any sense when some people say, "There is no truth," because they are really denying this higher category. It is also a performative contradiction, because the moment you say, "There is no truth," you make a universal truth claim and contradict yourself.

The Principle of Noncontradiction

Principles are beginnings; they are the point from which other things have their origin. A person has principles if she has some deeply held convictions from which her actions flow. In philosophy, we have a number of such principles, too, and the most important one is called the principle of noncontradiction. It sounds a bit intimidating, but believe me, it is very simple.

When we begin to discover the world, we grasp one truth very early on—namely, the difference between *being* and *nonbeing*. When you are hungry and sit in front of an empty plate, and you know that there is no food on it, you grasp the difference between something and nothing, between being and nonbeing. The principle of noncontradiction, something Aristotle wrote about over two thousand years ago, is that something cannot *be* and *not be* at the same time and in the same respect. The computer on which I write these lines cannot exist and not exist at the same time and under the same respect. Someone could claim that from a quantum perspective, the computer might not actually be there but just appear to be so—and I would simply say, well, okay, but that is from a different perspective, which is not the same respect.

This principle is the basis for all our knowledge because we can only know things that exist, either in our mind (like math) or in the real world (like stones or people). Without it, we could not communicate with each other because our words would not make sense. Nothing would.

Now you probably wonder whether we can prove this principle of noncontradiction—no, we can't. That's the point of principles: they are beginnings, and we can go no further. Everything you come up with to back up the principle presupposes it already, and everything you write or think about it is only possible because of it! So, we can say that the principle is the foundation of all our knowledge and communication, but it is so basic that we cannot prove it because it is the basis for everything else.

Can I Be a Skeptic?

One school of philosophy, the so-called skeptics, called all truth into question. Very similar to the example above, they denied that we can arrive at any truth and overlooked that they contradicted themselves. Skepticism never really went away and occasionally resurfaced in various forms. Most common today is the skepticism about truth claims and the denial that there is any *objective* truth.

You see there is a slight difference. The modern skeptics have learned that they have to change their agenda a bit. So instead of denying truth altogether, they deny that there is *objective* truth, but they overlook the fact that their propositions claim to be *objective*! You can't deny that the cake exists and then eat two pieces of it!

One of the most famous philosophers, Descartes, even doubted the foundation of his whole philosophy. He thought that we should be doubtful of everything until we find an unshakable basis for our thoughts. For example, what if I am wrong to believe that the world exists? Descartes said that even if I am deceived by every-thing, since I am the one who reasons, and who is deceived, the existence of this thinking "I" is the unshakable, first principle of all knowledge.

This sounds at first convincing, but could it be that Descartes overlooked that he presupposed the law of noncontradiction, and thus the famous phrase "I think, therefore I am" cannot be the first principle? After all, he didn't take into consideration that the world exists *and* does not exist at the same time. He rather presupposed two contradicting truth claims (either the world ex-ists *or* it does not) and also missed that one could doubt doubting itself. So even Descartes could not find a better starting point for philosophy and relied on the highest principles of thinking, for which we cannot give proofs. It obviously bothered Descartes that such principles would exist, because they require acceptance and trust, but perhaps that is the sign of true wisdom, to accept for the highest principles something that you cannot prove but that is the foundation of everything you think. The reliance of humans on these principles might also serve as a clue that our approach to reality should be one not of skepticism but rather of acceptance and trust.[3]

How Many Does It Take?

How many people does it take to make something true? Odd question, right? Have you never known someone to make a claim and back it up by saying, "Everybody says so"? Let's play around with that thought for a bit. For example, many people buy clothes according to fashion trends, based on what is in style right now and what is not. Those are judgments about fashion, and that is not what I am talking about. What I am referring to here are *moral judgments*. Moral statements are truth claims.

Let's consider the ethical rule that stealing is immoral. This is an objective truth claim, and if we deny it, then we are denying a moral truth. Does it matter how many people think stealing is bad? Not really, because even if the whole world suddenly decided it was a great idea, it wouldn't change the moral truth. However, peer pressure is real, and even if we think we are independent individuals, research shows that almost everybody caves to the will of the crowd at some point.

It is important to note that although stealing is objectively immoral, there are a few exceptions to this rule. Although personal property is valuable, and protecting it provides peace and stability in a society, human life trumps it. A person in danger of starving can licitly steal to provide for his or her most basic needs. After World War II, the ethicist and archbishop of Cologne rightly excused his flock for stealing coal to heat their homes or stealing potatoes to feed their struggling families.[4]

Some will jump on this and say that because there are exceptions to the rule, the moral truth claim about stealing was not objective. I would counter this objection by saying that the exception does *not* negate the fact that stealing, in *all non-life-or-death situations*, is immoral. In fact, it even emphasizes it!

Nevertheless, there are still people who argue that there are no objective moral norms and that we only make them up as we go along. If that is the case, let's see how this attitude applies to rape. I believe that there is never justification for rape and that there is no possible way in which rape could ever be moral. It is always immoral regardless of what world we live in. However, what if a majority of the population decided that it was not? Could rape then be moral in some instances? If you agree with me that no majority of people whatsoever could ever make rape moral, then you agree that there is at least one objective moral truth, and thus you agree that the statement "Rape is always immoral" is true. You have then implicitly agreed to the idea that there is truth independent from a majority of peers—but why?

It is here where true philosophy begins. Where does this moral truth come from? Why would I believe in things like human dignity and following moral laws? It only makes sense, some philosophers argue, if humans have inherent dignity and if moral laws are grounded in a higher truth—namely, God. If God as all-goodness exists, then there is an absolute standard of goodness, an absolute morality.

Using our reason, we found that rape is always immoral, and this finding is grounded in the existence of such a divine, all-good being. Science, on the other hand, cannot give a foundation for any moral claims, because it would be an overreach into philosophy.[5] Yet if there is *no* God, moral laws like "rape is immoral" have no basis; they are merely conventions: People agreed on them in certain societies and at certain times, but why could such a convention not change? If there is no God, then there is no foundation to morality, there are no objective moral laws at all. Again, do not misunderstand me! The atheist can be moral, but she has no ultimate reason to be, other than personal preference, convention, or survival. There is no "objective" and absolute good in her naturalist framework. Likewise, in the absence of God, suffering makes no sense—in particular, suffering inflicted by other human beings. The person believing in God will fight against injustice but will often lose such battles. Yet she knows that in God there is final justice that sets things right. The victims receive retribution, and the evildoers will be punished. The German philosopher Immanuel Kant, himself not the churchgoing type, therefore argued that only if we suppose God exists is there *hope*.

12

Real Thinking Discovers Causes

Understanding the reasons for things, their causes, gives us a glimpse into the core of reality and allows us the chance to acquire *true knowledge*. Understanding causes rests on the assumption that the world is intelligible and, furthermore, that things really are connected. The latter is most often under attack by philosophers who deny that we can discover true causality. Thus, empowering the mind requires us to demonstrate our ability to discover causes.

The Classic Four Causes

When we talk about *causes*, we usually think of *effect causality*, such as fire causing smoke, but the ancient philosophers argued that there are four types of causes: material, formal, efficient, and final. The first cause, according to Aristotle, is the material cause. A wooden table's material cause is the wood. The second is called its formal cause, which in our case is its "tableness"—because the form of "table" is different from the form of "chair" or "bookshelf." Material and formal causes *constitute* the object we are observing. Without them, the table would not exist. Yet the objects we observe are not static but subject to change; some begin to exist, some cease to exist, and some undergo modifications. Some also change their form. For example, lumber can be turned into a table, and a table can be recycled into wood pellets. An efficient cause refers to a relationship of dependence between two such forms; for example, in temporal affairs, one form appears first and the other later, such as lumber being turned into a table. In this case, the carpenter is the efficient cause because he makes the table out of the lumber. Another example of efficient cause would be God sustaining the universe in existence, because it is dependent on him. The final cause explains the purpose for which something exists (e.g., a table's final purpose is for people to sit at it and eat, write, etc.).

Do Things Just Pop into Existence?

Let's go back to efficient causality, which is all about change. Some say "there is no effect without a cause," but this statement does not elucidate much because when we use the word *effect*, we *presuppose* the existence of a *cause*. I think it is better to say that *everything that has a beginning must have a cause*. I don't think anyone would object to this.

It is important to note that not only things but also qualities, relationships, and ideas can have causes if they have a beginning in time. Something that brings another thing into existence is called a *cause*. We can easily observe this when we create a story in our mind or arrive at the solution to a mathematical problem. We bring something new into existence because we are causing it.

Yet how do we know that something that *appears* to be a cause is *really* a cause? After all, one could just say that we see one event, and then another event, but we cannot see the first event *causing* the second. We do not see the *inner tie* that connects cause and effect outside ourselves (we sense it when we cause things within us, though). For example, I see a billiard ball hit another ball, and then see that other ball moving around the table, but I do not see "causation" itself. Another example would be that I multiply 12 by 13 in my head. As a result, I become conscious of the number 156, which is different from the two other numbers. I perceive it and can point to the method of multiplication to explain how I arrived at it, but I do not perceive the "causation" of 156 or even a causal relation between the numbers and the end result.

The Scottish philosopher David Hume saw this correctly when he stated that we cannot *perceive* by *experience* a causal relation; yet he omitted that we can state such a relation by *reasoning*. Hume went further and explained that causality was due to the fact that our mind *associates* things that happen in a specific order of time and space (*first this, then that*). Thus we cannot refute Hume merely by saying, "But whenever we roll the ball into the other ball, it passes on that movement." After all, Hume would say that this is just how our mind works: it adds up experiences, but it tells us nothing about reality. Causation might just be an invention of our mind.[1]

What Hume missed, however, was that there is a profound bond between all the elements, a web of relations. He thought there were only timely and spatial relations between the elements. He smuggled into his argument the view that our mind would be forced to establish associations between things that happen repeatedly and only "construct" a bond between them. Because he thought the mind only perceived temporal and spatial impressions, he excluded that our mind could *reason* that one event *must* happen for the other event to come into existence, and that the second event always comes into being when the first happens. Hume's skepticism about causation thus rests on the idea that every event is preceded by one and followed by another. If these events happen repeatedly, the mind merely invokes the label *causality*, because it is forced to do so. Yet why would nature behave in such a way as to appease the demands of our mind? Why would nature be obedient to the demands of our mind and connect things in such and such a way? Hume never answered that question, and Immanuel

Kant also avoided it. After all, it shows that such reasoning is an artistic escape from realism. Is it not more reasonable to suppose that our mind *discovers* some aspects of the world, like the connections between things, and follows the rules of nature? The realist believes just that—while a Humean or Kantian must believe that nature, oddly enough, follows the structure of our mind!

Moreover, for Hume there are no abstract concepts such as *causation* but simply individual images and thoughts. This means that there is consequently no *real, profound* connection between things in the world (see the next section), because for that you need causation. For Hume, we can imagine things popping into existence without a cause because the things of the world are not really *connected*. The problem with this argument, however, is that he overlooked something: even if you imagine things coming into existence without a cause, you are connected to this thought!

Last but not least, when we *cause things ourselves*, we immediately grasp the power that brings things into existence—namely, our will and mind—and we wonder whether this experience is also valid in the world around us. If things that come into existence in my mind need a *sufficient reason*, or a cause, for their existence, do things outside my mind too?

Coming into Existence Needs a Cause

We could turn the previous statement around to better understand what it means *to cause something*. Would it be possible for something that began to exist to have *never* come into existence?[2] For example, the universe exists now (after all we know now, it began to exist at a distant moment in the past), so was it possible that it *never* came into existence? If you say no, you seem to imply that the universe exists by necessity—and then you would face the question of what the root for that necessity would be (see the section on necessity below). If you say yes (it could also not have come into existence), you face this question: Why did it come into existence? Now, you could say it just happened, and we will consider this "popping into existence" idea below, but you could also say that something *caused* it into existence. If it has a cause, then you can still ask whether this cause brought the universe by necessity into being, like two chemicals necessarily cause a reaction.

If this sequence was *necessary*, then we must further ask *why*, because every necessity must be grounded in something. This ground cannot be *in* the thing that has come into existence (universe), because the ground predates the effect. So there has to be something from which this necessity, this "must," comes and which brings the new thing "universe" into existence. Something is a cause insofar as it is the ground for such a must.

Why do we have to talk about necessity? Couldn't we just deny that it matters at all? We could, but then we would still have to answer why something came into existence in the first place. Some philosophers say we shouldn't bother asking the question of *why* the universe came into existence but should simply take it as a fact. Things come into existence *without* causes, they claim, and Bertrand Russell even famously said that for all we know, the universe could have just popped into existence five minutes ago.[3] The reasoning behind it is clear: if I believe that things that began to exist need a cause, then I ultimately have to ask what brought the universe, space, and time into being.

Of course, we know of the Big Bang or the great singularity in which time and space have their origin. Thus, one cannot ask what was *before* the Big Bang, because time began with it. Nevertheless, one can ask what *caused* it, and why. When I do that, I quickly arrive at a cause for everything that exists, which philosophers have usually called *God*. Since this cause would be the ground for all existence, it cannot be material itself. If God exists, he is the reason for all that exists, but he is not an existing *thing* in time or space. Asking for a cause of all existence, asking for a cause of the Big Bang, was meaningless for Russell. If one asks that question, he thought, one would permit the uncomfortable God-question. Nevertheless, I find it intellectually dissatisfying to stop short of asking for the cause of something (like the universe) that clearly has a beginning.[4]

It is noteworthy, however, that many philosophers rejected Russell's idea of uncaused things popping into existence. G. E. M. Anscombe, for example, probably the greatest female philosopher of the twentieth century, detected a flaw in Russell's argument. After all, how can we even reasonably state that they pop "into existence"? Could they not have been transferred from another space and time? She proved that we can distinguish between things that are transported in such a way and things that pop into existence only if we have a concept of causation. Thus, in trying to eliminate the principle of causation, even Russell has to assume it for his own argument![5]

If we give up the principle of causation (that everything that comes into existence has a cause), it becomes awfully hard to explain the existence of the universe. After all, if we follow Russell, there must be things that begin to exist but are *not* dependent on a cause. Instead, they must carry the reason for their existence in themselves and thus be *necessary*.

Of course, Russell, as we explained above, *denies* that necessity must have a grounding. Nevertheless, if these things are really the reason for their own existence, they must be absolutely *independent* from all other beings (nothing can influence them and thus inflict causation on them). And finally, such "necessary" things must also be able to pop *out of existence* at any point in time without any cause. They come from nothing and vanish into nothing, totally uncaused. I don't know what you think about this, but I find Russell's thoughts impossible to reconcile with the world as we know it. Is this not just a highly sophisticated argument to avoid the God-question? If not, I cannot see how eliminating causation either helps foster scientific progress or enables human responsibility.

One aspect that bothers me perhaps the most is that Russell needs to presuppose that things are independent and somehow totally secluded from each other. Each thing is its own cosmos, so to speak. Yet you and I can observe that the world is a complicated ecosystem in which *everything* is connected. Even the universe itself is not a group of independent things floating in space but rather a web of *relations*. After all, do we not acknowledge that even though the earth is a "whole," it is also part of a greater thing called the universe that influences all kinds of circumstances on this planet? If we believe, as Russell did, that things pop into existence that are absolutely independent from each other, how can such a whole with relationships of dependence pop into existence? The only way to defend this view would be to embrace Russell's idea that *everything* just popped into existence, including our memories and our understanding of causality. And we saw above how problematic that would be!

Russell's idea might be a fun thought experiment, but if it is only in place to avoid the God-question at the price of sacrificing the principle of causation, it is not worth following. If we want to live in a world that is explainable and in which things relate to each other, influence each other, and have causes, Aristotle will lead us farther than Russell does.[6]

Do Things Pop out of Existence?

Everything that exists in the world is somehow connected to time and remains in *this* (temporal) condition *unless* it is changed by a *third* factor. The same seems to be true for things that do *not* exist: they are in a relationship to time insofar as they are not affected by it because they are only potentially existing, and they remain unrealized unless something actualizes them. (The tree is a *potential* chair until it is cut down and processed in a sawmill and by a carpenter.) We should be cautious to never forget this *third* factor, because otherwise we get a lopsided view of reality.

A thing *persists* in existence and needs a cause that influences it to cease existing. Likewise, something that comes newly into existence needs a cause for its realization. If we, however, adopt the view that things pop into existence, we cut ourselves off from explaining why things have some kind of *permanence*, why they last and need a cause to cease existing. It leads us to stop asking questions and, ultimately, stops our scientific progress because it prevents us from gaining more knowledge of our material world.

The aging of our bodies is a good example. A number of factors converge to cause our bodies to age and thus, ultimately, cause our death. Yet by understanding *our permanence* we better understand these factors and, in turn, ourselves. We talked already about the experience of the permanence of reality when we mentioned the experience of *resistance*: If I hit my head against the wall, it causes me pain, and I realize that something resists me. Unless a third factor eliminates the wall (perhaps some dynamite), it will remain exactly where it was when I bumped into it. The same applies in reverse to things that do not exist; in order for them to come into being, there must be a third factor, or power, that raises them up out of nothingness.

Where does this leave us? Our reasoning does not prove the principle of causality, but it does show that *we cannot reason without* it and that it is unlikely that nature would be merely an obedient follower of *our* thoughts. If we deny causality, we not only fail to explain the world but also will have serious problems surviving in it because to deny causality would be to deem the world an unexplainable jumble of events. However, if we grant the validity of causality, we are pushed to ask ourselves *what* brought *everything* into existence. As Stephen T. Davis once said, the honest rational answer to the latter question is the existence of God.[7]

Potency and Change

When we ask what constitutes the things of the world, the philosopher means something different than the physicist does. The physicist talks about molecules, atoms, electrons, neutrons, and so forth, but the philosopher has a different perspective. Remember, the philosopher is interested in what *being* means, what the abstract nature of a wave is, what the abstract nature of time is, and so forth. So the philosopher asks questions that cannot be answered by using the scientific method. The philosopher is interested in the nonmaterial factors that allow even material things (and immaterial ones) to exist.

Some of the things we encounter in our lives can be easily changed or manipulated, like clay, while others are more resistant to change, such as people. Even the universe changes every moment, yet it does not seem to have the ability to self-initiate such changes; instead, it seems dependent on causes that bring those effects about.

People, however, can "own" themselves and be self-initiated "movers": they have the power to undergo self-chosen change and have a will, have freedom. Yet as persons, we are also tied to physical bodies. Thus, it is only reasonable to suspect some influences of the body on our will. In fact, it seems that some physical influences can even overthrow our freedom and willpower (such as certain drugs).

When we carefully observe our own bodies and minds, all of us can realize different grades of "owning ourselves," of endurance in change, of self-chosen attitudes, or of suffering something inflicted upon us (like aging). That we all change seems therefore beyond any doubt, yet is there something in us that remains the same? Isn't it the case that old people tell us "I still feel young although I am eighty!"? Why is that? Although all of our cells are replaced every few years, there is something underneath our bodily existence that endures through all the change around it and remains the same. Such a thing of endurance and permanence the philosopher calls a *substance*.

Substances vary according to their participation in self-ownership as described above. The substance of the universe lacks the self-determination a person has. For example, a rabbit might have such a substance but is not aware of it like a human being is. Therefore, philosophers have traditionally called the highest form of substance an *intelligent, rational soul*. Philosophers call it an *accident* when anything attaches to a substance—for example, height or eye color—and gives it additional characteristics but is not necessary.

One of the toughest questions is *how* things change and how to explain what change is. If something changes, it brings about something new, but nevertheless this new thing was already there. That seems to be a contradiction, but bear with me. Change, one could say, is making present what was previously only *potentially* there. For example, a tree is a substance that is actualized (*exists*) but could *potentially* be a chair. The chair is somehow present within the tree but not realized. It needs a third factor, such as a sawmill and a carpenter, to bring it about.

If we keep this observation in mind, we might wonder what *kind* of substances remain in a certain condition unless they are changed by others. Connecting this to our findings about the *soul*, we realize that the rational soul is the only substance that moves and changes *itself*, while all others need a third factor, a cause, to bring them from one state into another. A tree never naturally becomes a chair, and when it dies and rots, a third factor (*decay*) imposes this change on the tree. Change, therefore, is strangely something we are suffering but also something we as persons with a rational soul can supremely "own." We seem to be the only substances in the universe able to change ourselves!

If we observe the world carefully, we realize that everything *in it*[8] has the potential to be something else, has the potential to change. Something that can change, however, is not perfect, because its susceptibility to change means there is some potential in it that has not been actualized. For example, I am potentially much faster in running a mile, but I am not right now. My athletic ability could be improved and thus lacks perfection. Everything finite lacks such a piece of perfection because it always contains some unrealized potential. (For example: "Thing *A* could be in place *B*." Even that is a potential not actualized!)

The whole world, as well as the universe, is constituted by things in *actuality* (actualized) and *potentiality* (potential). Everything that changes must first exist so that another aspect of it can be actualized. The question is not whether the chicken or the egg came first, because both are actualized beings, but rather what was first: something actual or only a possibility? Nothing comes from nothing, as we saw above, so a potential chicken never becomes real without a real, existing egg.

Yet philosophers have wondered whether there is one thing that has no potentiality in it, something that cannot change because it's perfect. This "something" would be perfection itself. Thomas Aquinas thought that if God exists, he is just that: *actus purus*, existence and perfection in its fullest form.

13

Thinking about Goods, Values, and Morality

I once asked a man why he stole a book from the library. His response was, "It felt right." This idea has become the universal ethics of today. Certainly, there is some truth to the idea that we "feel" something when we make an important decision, but what the person described has more depth. It is the idea that there are *no objective moral standards* and that if my feelings tell me something is good (even in cases where it clearly is not), then it must be so. When we base ethical decisions on emotions, however, we are not basing them on reason, and I think that is a major problem. Why?

Emotions Are Not about Truth

I am by nature an emotional person, so I am far from rejecting this important side of our personality. What I am trying to argue for, though, is that our emotions cannot be the foundation for our behavior.

First of all, emotions are fickle; they come and go. Having two teenage sons and a middle-school daughter at home, I have a first-row seat to the theater of hormone-based emotional roller coasters. Testosterone spikes contribute to aggression, and hormone fluctuations to rapidly changing emotions. It's not all that different with adults, just a bit more subdued.

Second, emotions are individual and cannot be the basis for universal rules of behavior. We live in societies and need to behave in certain ways to ensure the flourishing of our communities. We need rules. In what world would it make sense to base a universal code of conduct on feeling okay about stealing a book? It is based on me and *me* alone. Would it not mean some kind of imperialism to force it upon others? Moreover, is there any consideration of the common good in my emotions?

Do you think that is a bit harsh? I don't think so. Morality based on emotions is called *emotivism*. It eclipses reason because it denies that you have to give "reasons" for your actions that the rest of us can understand. We give reasons for our actions so that others can understand what we do and why we act in a certain way; reasons are an understandable way of communicating our motivations and decisions.

Reasons are used to justify our actions, but they also testify that we are committed to *accepting responsibility* for our actions. When I give, as a reason for stealing wood, that I need it to heat the house for my family, who would otherwise have frozen to death, I am committing myself to a line of thought and conduct that can be judged and evaluated by others. By expecting others to justify their actions as well, we can construct societal norms of behavior that ensure responsible conduct in the future.[1]

Compare this to an intuition-based or emotion-based morality: by definition, we cannot truly understand someone's emotions. We might have similar emotions, but *never* the same. A person who does what she "feels" is right cannot communicate motivations for her actions because they are in principle inaccessible to us. Her moral responsibility is to herself and not to others. The emotivist does not even accept the most basic rule of society that in order to thrive, we need to give rational justifications for our actions, to commit to an idea of responsibility and thus to a common good.

Yet what if there were no objective, universal moral rules? Wouldn't this make emotivism acceptable? Declaring the absence of any universal rule and then reintroducing a moral code through the back door doesn't make any sense. After all, if there is no universal morality that binds us all (even if just in very rough principles), then emotivism cannot be universal, either. That would be a contradiction! The very same has to be said about all moral theories that deny *any* objective, universal moral laws. To claim that there is no universal moral law is to establish one at the same time.

The Rational Foundation of Morality

Morality needs a rational foundation. Reason is available to all human beings, and therefore moral rules are, in principle, understandable by everyone who can think. We all desire happiness and things that fulfill us in various ways. These things philosophers call *goods*. Moral philosophy or ethics helps us to identify whether these goods are in conflict with the goods of others (for example, my neighbor or my wife) and what actions we are allowed to take to achieve them. For example, if I want to build a chicken coop, such a desire might be in conflict with the wish of my wife to keep our landscaping intact. And if I built it overnight without her knowledge or approval, such action would be immoral.

In moral philosophy we have to think about our actions and their ends. A number of philosophers have argued that there is a final end to human life, such as communion with God or moral perfection. Our actions are moral when they advance us toward this goal and immoral when they lead us away from it. The key is to search for and find our final end and to keep it continuously on our minds, especially before making important decisions.

There are different kinds of goods. Some goods we desire only for the sake of a greater good. For instance, my air conditioner recently broke. For the hot and humid summer months, I want to have a cool house, but in the winter, that will change because then I will want to have a well-heated living room. Therefore, the good I desire is not the cool or hot air but being comfortable in my home, which is necessary for my family to live and flourish. That is the higher good behind my desire for a new air conditioner. Other desires can be goods in themselves, like a loving family, or people, such as my wife and children. I cherish them not because of something they give me but for who they are. They are ends in themselves, not a means to an end.

However, it is not enough that I know an end or a good. I really have to desire it and make judgments about the means to obtain it. To desire a happy marriage is one thing; to achieve it is another. It's the same with all other goods in life. We can choose to pursue them through moral or immoral means, but then we must live with the consequences of those choices. If we based our actions merely on emotions, we would never achieve final ends because we wouldn't even know about them. We would be forever caught up in drives and passions alone. Reason is what saves us from that.

Goods such as friendship and love can also be called *values*, or things we consider worth pursuing. They are so intriguing to our affections and minds that we think they *should* exist. This "should" is the miracle of morality because only human minds discover "shoulds." When we say that spouses *should* love each other, for example, we are expressing a value. We claim that the good is universal and *should* be realized.

Philosophers of value, such as Max Scheler, have found that there are at least three groups of values: moral, aesthetic, and religious. The remarkable thing, however, is that although values express things which "should be realized," they do not tell us *how* to bring them about.[2]

People, however, often talk about their value systems or personal values, which reveals a problem with value-based ethics. Some can perceive values where others cannot—for example, in the beauty of a painting or a piece of music. If values exist independently from my mind and are objective—as, for example, Dietrich von Hildebrand argued—then I have to be able to explain why some people cannot perceive certain values. For him, people who continuously make immoral choices starve their souls from perceiving higher goods. In doing so, they become *value-blind*.[3]

Hildebrand's assertion might be true, and some psychological findings seem to support it, but I still find it intellectually unsatisfying. After all, if someone does not agree with me about a certain value, it doesn't do much good to charge him with being value-blind. I fear that this is often the case in our polarized society today. We call people who hold a different worldview or belong to a different party "closed minded" because they are unable to understand our "values." A much better way would be to lay out *what* has led us to believe that our values are self-evident. In doing so, we should try to visualize, using words, the horizon of our thinking and *why* and *how* the values we believe in appear in it. Any other way, I think, just perpetuates polarization. Most value-philosophers agree that we should test our values by discussing them with peers in order to make sure that we have not missed an important consideration or that we are not heading in the wrong direction. Reading value-philosophies, therefore, reminds me to be honest about what I claim as *evident* and to be patient with those who cannot follow me.[4]

I began this chapter by asking about universal moral laws, which are rules for human actions that are valid for everyone, regardless of time and space. Many will say that such universal or objective laws or standards do not exist because circumstances change over the course of history. Humanity changes. Historical and social changes certainly demonstrate that human behavior varies tremendously, but I do think that we can identify actions that are always good or evil. Rape is a horrible violation of a person, and rape is always immoral, in every situation, regardless of circumstances, in every possible world. If you agree, then you are no longer a relativist. You are someone who accepts that there are some very basic universal moral laws, such as not harming the physical and psychological integrity of a human person. There may not be many such moral principles, and I think they do exist. The emotivist can be outraged about rape or discrimination, but he has no rational standard on which he bases his emotion. He cannot say rape or torture is universally wrong, because he does not believe in universal moral laws.

Human beings are rational animals. We form bonds with one another not only for instrumental purposes, such as being a friendly neighbor or a good colleague, but also because we grasp that there are relationships that matter deeply for our personal fulfillment and development. They make us think about the big question of life, its meaning and final end. If we do not want to see people and the world only through the lens of how useful they are to us (*utilitarianism*) or how they make us feel, then we should consider *natural law theory*.

The philosophy of natural law claims that there are some very basic absolute principles of morality and universal objective goods, such as friendship, love, virtue, and above all the dignity of the thinking, free human person. The most basic principle of natural law besides "One should always do good and avoid evil" can be expressed this way: "Act always in a way that is conducive to integral human fulfillment or at least compatible with it."

Most of the other principles of morality that can be applied to concrete situations follow from these two principles. It is important, however, to understand that *integral fulfillment* requires more than merely satisfying material needs such as food, clean water, shelter, and bodily integrity.

If we recognize that the human person as a rational animal is able to obtain *bits* of absolute *truth* and has an immaterial mind (and most likely even a soul), intellectual and spiritual well-being *must* be included under integral fulfillment as well. Once we have grasped this, we can better understand the weight and importance of human rights as principles that should guide our actions. We respect them not because they are useful for us but because they are true and good and can never be justly suspended by any demand of politics or economics.

Natural law philosophers are convinced about the objective reality of such principles and goods, though they vary in how both are known and implemented.[5]

14

Thinking Saves Lives

"That is so impractical!" say some when they hear you talk about reasoning and philosophy. "I prefer to live!" Diligent thinking is often dismissed like this because it requires stamina. It is like lifting weights. The more you have trained, the more weight you can lift. However, most will legitimize their dismissal with the profound prejudice that thinking has no practical impact on people's lives. Therefore, it is a waste of time and should be avoided, they say. I have encountered this attitude many times. In this chapter I will show why it is utterly false and how thinking can make your life better.

First, we must distinguish daydreaming from thinking. Imagining a world in which I win the lottery or become an NFL star might be fun and entertaining, but it is not thinking. Such daydreams are free-floating soap bubbles that pop at their first encounter with reality. Daydreaming is neither practical nor life changing, apart from the fact that it might relax you for a while.

Intentional Perception

Real thinking, as we have already seen, is *focused* on something. We can stare at the world as long as we want to, but we won't get any smarter or better until we narrow our focus, find an object, and put the spotlight of our reason on it. Then miracles can happen. Confucius supposedly said that everything has its beauty, but not everyone can see it. Much depends on our capacity for intentional perception.

A good example of intentionality is *prospective memory*. It means that we intentionally remember to do certain *future* actions. Professors are, of course, known to be absentminded, and I have forgotten my fair share of things, but I am trying to train my prospective memory by forming very clear intentions for my life. Instead of saying that I will do better tomorrow, I tell myself that tomorrow "I will respond to all incoming emails" or "I will not forget to close the garage door." Such specificity trains your prospective (future) memory. By giving our mind a future object to focus on, we create a fixed point of orientation for the next day or near future.

Human beings have the unique capacity to construct goals, which spur us into action. Goals are things we want. They must be achievable (otherwise they are just dreams), and they must be precisely identified (otherwise they will be forgotten). We have to have a goal or destination in mind before we can think about how we will achieve it. For both tasks, we need to think carefully and follow the rules of logic.

Psychologists have long observed that people with lots of self-control are more successful and have wondered why. Is it because they are better at resisting strong temptations and can form better routines, which enable them to achieve their goals? Perhaps, but the latest research suggests that highly disciplined people are also better at *identifying* and *choosing* goals that reflect their true self, while people with less self-control choose goals that culture projects onto them. Thus, to a large extent, success boils down to *being realistic* about our abilities and goals.

People who think about their goals tend to align them with their values and abilities. Diligent thinking allows them to make the goals intelligible and to develop mechanisms of self-control.

When we lack serious thinking, however, we tend to avoid constraints and discipline and lead less successful and fulfilling lives.[1]

Psychologists have found that such diligent thinking—which identifies the right goals, mechanisms of self-control, and ends—can be trained by concentrating on specific future tasks. Instead of merely stating a vague summer project we want to accomplish, it is infinitely better to make specific plans and develop detailed goals. This stimulates our cognitive faculties, and our mind shifts to a more active mode. Such *episodic future thinking*, like prospective memory on steroids, makes it more likely not only that you will remember those goals but also that you will successfully accomplish them. A lot depends on the strength of the images we associate with our plans. The less detailed and colorful they are, the less successful they will be.

This method of planning is not so different from the meditation technique Ignatius of Loyola suggests in his *Spiritual Exercises* to those making a spiritual retreat.[2] The founder of this religious order taught his followers to immerse themselves in a biblical passage by imagining all its details. His disciples were instructed to see themselves in the biblical episode and to use all their senses to comprehend what was going on. Over the course of thirty days, these meditations led to a clear imagination of one's future engagement in the service of Jesus and of one's own vocation. The impressions of such a retreat, Ignatius believed, would last a lifetime.[3] Like future episodic thinking, the *Spiritual Exercises* use imagination to identify and impress certain goals (one's vocation, following God's commands, etc.) onto our memory and emotions. Yet both warn that imagination is a tool that has to be used in a *disciplined* way. Imagination is not mere daydreaming but a *concentrated effort* of the mind based on reason. After all, reason reminds us to train our intentions but also keeps us from letting imagination wreak havoc in our life.

Daydreaming is not a rational use of imagination. Instead, it is without any intentional object, a mere drifting of thoughts and

(handwritten at top: ① Do you think your irrational beliefs are holding you back from something?)

thus deeply *irrational*. That's why we call it *dreaming*. Dreams are never coherent, because we do not intend them—they happen to us due to our subconscious. Therefore, the oddest things happen in our dreams—things that contradict the laws of nature and logic. When we dream, our intentionality (the focusing power of our mind) is subdued, and we float above reality like a cloud pushed by the wind. We have to go wherever the dream takes us. Future episodic thinking and Ignatian meditation, however, are grounded in intentionality, reality, and the power of reason.

Besides future episodic thinking, reason can also help us deal with irrational beliefs that overshadow our lives and make us miserable. Consider the employee who constantly believes she is undervalued although she gets many promotions, or the business owner who believes the entire world is out to destroy his enterprise, or the woman who has terrible interview anxiety even though she is skilled and qualified. These people's *irrational beliefs* influence their emotions and make them feel bad. These beliefs influence their behavior and can lead to poor choices. The question is, What makes their beliefs irrational? I bet you already have some *ideas*, and that is exactly the point: reason helps us check our beliefs to see whether they are corresponding to reality or not.

Disputing Irrational Beliefs

It is here where psychology and philosophy meet. Beginning in the 1960s, psychologists rediscovered the power of reasoning and made it a cornerstone for *rational-emotive behavior therapy*. Albert Ellis has suggested that reasonable beliefs are those that help us succeed in our projects, while those that are irrational emotionally disturb us because they contain empirical distortions or exaggerated evaluations of ourselves or the world.[4]

Ellis's main point, it seems, was that irrational beliefs are false evaluations of the world and of ourselves, pushed to an extent that makes us sick.[5] While many psychologists are not content with this, I think it is sufficient for our purposes at hand. Reason helps us discover the world, but when our perceptions are distorted, this distortion leads to *false evaluations* and *irrational beliefs*. Some of the latter, however, might not be worth challenging because they do not have a huge influence on our well-being, just as some rational beliefs (e.g., about the veracity of logical laws) might not either. So, let's find out whether we can detect the irrational beliefs in our lives that affect us negatively.

I once met a young woman who had graduated from an Ivy League school, had a great job, and was happily married with children but believed herself to be a failure. "I feel worthless and alone. Nobody could ever love me. Why am I even alive?" An outside observer would have detected that everything in this woman's life was pointing to success and happiness, except her own self-evaluation. How could she have such a distorted view of herself? Her beliefs were formed when she was emotionally abandoned by her parents, she told me later, but it was *philosophical reasoning* that saved her.

Irrational beliefs such as self-loathing, feelings of unworthiness, and many anxieties can be defeated with the power of proper thinking. Rational-emotive behavior therapy suggests that constantly *disputing* irrational beliefs with logical thinking leads to a replacement of the destructive beliefs with rational ones, which has a positive influence on our behavior. Instead of seeing yourself as hated by everyone, you will come to see that you are in reality loved by some and treated with benign indifference by most. Instead of the black-and-white pattern of overgeneralizing the world and exaggerating our evaluations, we become emotionally sober. Irrationality is a bit like being drunk, because you cannot see the world as it is, and we have to jump into the cold shower of reason to wake up to reality.

The way to do this is by disputing irrational beliefs. *Disputation* was the way in which academics discussed their arguments for thousands of years. Originally, it meant to consider things *separately* from each other; only later was it applied to arguments. Disputing things is a way to *disentangle* the chaotic knot within our psyche. We have to excavate each wire and label it. Only once we have done that can we see how they are connected. Then, however, the hard work really begins, because now that we have discovered a certain irrational belief, such as "I have to feel happy all the time," we have to actively argue against it. Ellis found that a good approach to disputing such beliefs was to demand empirical evidence for them. Once we can see that they do not have a foundation in reality, we use logic to question the irrational belief itself.

"How does it logically follow that because I want to be happy, I have to be happy *at all times*? Is there a connection between my strong desire to feel happy and the *necessity* of having it always? Does my belief stem from this?"[6] A person who has studied philosophy can answer this question better than someone who hasn't. After all, a philosophy student learns about what follows from presuppositions, about conclusions, and about what makes things necessary. A person who is actively training her mind will see connections that another person misses and will be able to question herself and the world more honestly. The more powerful your logic is and the more you have trained your brain, the more successful you will be in battle. And it is a fight, because you are trying to change a deep-seated belief. One can only root it out successfully after a long siege.

We can strengthen this logical approach by giving it a more pragmatic goal—namely, by considering "What does this belief get me?" This is not merely pragmatic, because identifying an *achievable goal* is something we do with our *mind*, with reason and will. Proper thinking that is grounded in reality will help us check if we are dreaming or caught up in irrational beliefs.

Rational-emotive behavior therapy can change lives and refocus the mind so that it can let go of anxieties that lead to depression or even suicidal thoughts. It has helped countless people suffering from PTSD and improved the quality of their lives. "It made me want to live again," as one person who underwent such therapy told me. The next time someone tells you that thinking is impractical, you know what to tell them.

15

Empathy Is Achieved by Hard Thinking

A very close friend of mine was recently diagnosed with dementia. While he took the news bravely, I seemed to take the news harder than he did. I began to think about what life will be like for him, and I wondered whether I have been empathetic enough to the people around me who have similar challenges. When I told a philosopher friend about my soul-searching, he said, "If you are wondering whether you are empathetic enough, you clearly have empathy. Otherwise, that question would not occur to you!"

Walking in Somebody Else's Shoes

As reassuring as this was, I went to the library and tried to read what philosophers had to say about the subject. I read medieval and modern philosophy, but nothing really clicked with me. After all, I wanted to know whether empathy had a rational basis and whether it was somehow connected to my thinking. When I began researching the works of Max Scheler and Edmund Husserl, two twentieth-century German philosophers, I realized I was getting closer to some answers, but I felt intellectually unsatisfied until I read Edith Stein's *On the Problem of Empathy*.

Stein was an extraordinary woman and one of the most fascinating thinkers of the twentieth century. She overcame numerous obstacles and became one of the first women to earn a doctorate in philosophy. As a student of Husserl, she practiced *phenomenology*. This is a specific philosophical approach dedicated to discovering secure knowledge about objects present to our consciousness. These are things in *themselves*, untainted by personal experience. How, for example, is friendship present to *everyone's* consciousness? In order to arrive at such knowledge, one has to strip away everything personal and fallible from this mental impression (for example, all of *my* personal images of friendship) and any connection to friendships existing in the world. Layer after layer is peeled away, so that in the end you arrive at the *essence* of friendship in general.[1] Stein's doctoral project aimed at discovering nothing less than the essence of *empathy*.[2]

Since for most people empathy means feeling someone else's feelings, it requires us to somehow sense the other person's interior life. How do we do that? And is that even possible? When I see a downtrodden friend, I might recognize her pain, but the pain she feels is not perceivable to me in the way her face is. Her first-person experience is not communicable to me. Nevertheless, I still sense her pain—but how?

First, let us be clear about what I do not mean by empathy. It does not mean that I notice changes in a person, such as sad facial expressions, and then conclude that someone is in pain. This would be a *mere observation* and has no connection to my inner life, and when I "feel" empathy, it certainly does not feel like a cold observation. It also does not mean that I *merely associate* the impression of my friend with my own memory of pain, my first-person experience, because that would not be empathy either. It would merely be the projection of my own experience onto another person. The same applies to my imagination because merely imagining another's feelings is another form of projecting something onto them.

Instead, Edith Stein argues that the only way empathy can be more than our own projections is when it reaches the inner self of the other person. It is the experience of another person's *inner life*, and it involves becoming *aware of another person's consciousness*. It happens in three steps. In the first step, I encounter my friend and perceive sadness in him, perhaps because he looks sad. Then, I avoid making this sadness the object of my own experience, instead allowing it to draw me in so that I am close to the friend and take his position (so that I can be fully present to what my friend is experiencing). This second step is, however, more than just listening. It is an attentive "feeling into" the other person that avoids making the sadness of my friend my own. Instead, it is an *attentive awareness* of the other's suffering and means getting lost in his experience and perspective.[3]

What Stein calls "feeling into" seems similar to the full attention we give someone we love in a time of need. In such moments, we don't reason back and forth but throw ourselves with all our attention at the feet of the other. We are with him without paying attention to ourselves. Only in the third step do I form the experience of step two into an object of my reflection. Then I realize what I have felt and am able to differentiate the experience of the other from my own.

Step two, however, is only possible because the other person has, like me, an immaterial soul. Our souls are what allow us to be fully present to the other, forget ourselves, and assume the viewpoint of the person we are trying to reach.[4] This comes very close to what John Henry Newman had in mind when he stated, "*Cor ad cor loquitur*" ("Heart speaks to heart"). We can pay such undivided attention and gain another person's perspective only because we have souls.

In an act of empathy, I am completely with the other. That means that if I focus my attention on experiences of pain and joy *in myself*, perhaps as a result of my friend's misfortune, then these experiences have their *origin in me*, and I have already lost connection with the experience of the other. Thus, when someone says, "Oh, your experience makes me sad," the danger is that he focuses on the feeling in himself rather than on the other person. For Stein, this becomes even worse when we cultivate such a feeling because we think it is virtuous. We want to feel the pain of the other and concentrate on the sadness it causes in us, but by doing so we actually betray the other because we are only chasing our emotions. True empathy is therefore not about *my* experiences and feelings but about perceiving and *accepting* those of another. If we follow this analysis, most of what passes for empathy nowadays is just emotion hunting and not real empathy.

In the moments we truly act out of empathy, we "lose ourselves" in the other, and it is only in hindsight that we can see whether we have acted in empathy. I think that is a rather important observation: like love or friendship, empathy loses itself in the other. Thus our attention should not be so much on *intending empathy*, because this easily creates psychological pressure and distracts us from paying attention to the person we should be empathizing with! What we can intend, however, is paying attention to the *other* whose state of soul we accept. Only then are we able to sense someone's joy or pain and comprehend it. The following third step is a reflection on the previous steps, in which I realize that I have either felt empathy or not.

I found this analysis remarkable, because Stein liberates us from the false understanding that in order to be empathetic, we must feel a certain way or exactly like the other person. Too many people have felt pressured to feel something they cannot feel and consequently believed they lacked empathy. Others have cultivated emotion chasing to the extent that they became unable to perceive the joy and suffering of others. Virtue signaling is their special strength.

Instead, Stein invites us to see empathy as the ability to *be attentively with* another person. Careful reasoning like that of Edith Stein prevents us from becoming empathy hunters, who have to feel affected or outraged or overjoyed in the service of their own egos.

Self-Awareness Is Needed for Empathy

In order to be attentive to another person, we need to be aware of our own bodies. My body is the only thing that is always "here" and never absent, never "there." It is the basis for my "I," my point of orientation in the world, and the place from which I have a whole range of experiences.

Empathy, then, is a bit like taking on another body as a new basic point of orientation. I do that with reason, not emotion. I try to accept the world from the other person's perspective. Instead of discursive listening, where I register what I agree and disagree with, I just listen and accept. When your friend feels sad and expresses loneliness, don't make it about you but rather try to accept her perspective as your *basic point of orientation*. See the world like she does, and you will sense her pain. Practicing such attentiveness and acceptance is not easy and will probably be a lifelong struggle for most of us. Yet once you see how beautiful this substantial understanding of empathy is, you will never want to go back to the fluffy sentimentalist one.

For Edith Stein, true empathy modifies and corrects one's world-view. One worldview is enriched by the other, because we learn to see the world from a different angle. Therefore, empathy is not a negligible thing but the foundation for a healthy development of our mind. It enables us to grow and mature, to reach beyond the horizon of our own bodies and souls. Without it we could never share an experience with another person, and there would be no such things as *intersubjective* experience, as the philosopher calls it: we learn from each other through the empathetic act of our consciousness, but because we do it so rarely, we do not develop into the mature persons we could be. After all, empathy invites us to become aware of our own bodies, hopes, and desires, but also our own limitations and quirks. It takes time and can be exhausting, and it cannot be proudly displayed on social media.

Edith Stein's doctoral thesis was published in 1916. Months later, her insights were put to the test. Stein was close friends with a married couple named Adolf and Anna Reinach, and when Adolf died during the war, Edith was devastated by the news. She went to visit the Reinach family home and anticipated a grief-stricken widow, but she encountered something else. Although Anna Reinach loved her husband very much and was deeply saddened by his death, she felt a great inner peace. When Edith came to visit her, it was Edith, not Anna, who needed consolation. Anna and Adolf Reinach had previously converted to Christianity, and the widow found solace in her religion: in the cross, in the knowledge that God suffered with her and helped her to overcome her grief, and in the hope of a reunion in heaven. This was the moment when Stein realized that she would convert too. In 1942, Edith Stein died in the gas chambers of Auschwitz.[5]

Thinking about Emotions

While emotions should not be used to justify the morality of actions, they are an indispensable part of who we are, and thus we have to take them seriously. Some see emotion and reason as opposed to each other, but I have always found helpful the image from ancient philosophy that depicts feelings as powerful horses drawing a warrior's chariot, steered by personified "reason."

Feelings often happen to us, and they have the power to push our mind in ways we might not necessarily desire. Sometimes they confuse us. Because of this, we have to discover what these emotions mean and whether they contradict or support our life choices. If we don't do that, we run the risk of being driven by them, which will make it very difficult to create a stable existence for ourselves and to mature as persons. That is why philosophers have insisted for more than two thousand years that we should try to control our emotions and align them with our overall goals for fulfillment.

Some call the reign of reason over emotion "cold" because they see a lack of compassion in rational arguments. This is, however, a prejudice. After all, feelings are not necessarily friendly or compassionate. Humans are often more prone to selfish desire, anger, or the will to rule over others than to kindness or hospitality. Being informed by reason enables us to be compassionate because it reminds us that all people have dignity and value, no matter how we may feel about a particular individual or group. We cannot make feelings the guiding principle of our actions because they are unable to guide: they give us incoherent pushes in different directions but never a map to where we should go. Reason helps us control our emotions and makes us aware of their influence so that we can live stable, moral lives. Emotions positively influence our reasoning when they alert us to problems we might otherwise overlook, and they negatively influence our reasoning when they make us too cautious. In the end, the more carefully we observe our emotions, the better we will know ourselves and our reasoning process. We will become aware of a much wider emotional horizon and learn to reason through our emotions instead of being pushed around by them.

16

Leadership, Values, and Your Thoughts

From the Middle Ages to the French Revolution, books with titles such as *Mirror of the Prince* or *Mirror of the Good Judge* were legion. They were ethical guidebooks for leadership positions in society and church. It is only in the last few decades that we have rediscovered the ancient truth that true leadership depends on the morality of the leader. After all, the more power a person has, the more she can use it for good or evil purposes. You have to be a moral person to truly lead. It is a virtue! (This is not all that leadership requires.)

Characteristics of Leadership

Leaders have the ability to give careful, reasonable directives. This depends largely on the ability to properly judge what is within their power and what is not. One of the greatest military geniuses of all time was the Bohemian General Albrecht von Wallenstein. During the Thirty Years' War (1618–48), he commanded the greatest army the world had seen until then. Nobody could fathom how he had raised it. Moreover, his contemporaries despised him because his major strategy was never to engage in battle unless he was sure he would win. He knew exactly what his soldiers could and could not achieve. Wallenstein was no philosopher, but he

143

was trained in a classical high school curriculum, which included many philosophy and logic courses. Moreover, he owned some of the leadership manuals mentioned above. This education prepared him to identify opportunities, weigh options, and get to know his own powers and resources.

How so? The crucial tool of the philosophy of the time was the "distinction." If someone posed a problem, you dissected it into necessary and unnecessary parts. You made distinctions. This way of thinking, deeply ingrained in Wallenstein (and also in me), enables someone to differentiate without necessarily ripping things apart. *Distinguishing* is the fine art of seeing differences in the absence of obvious contradictions. It is a bit like identifying different shades of color without destroying a painting.

Another leadership characteristic is the ability to prepare for future events. One has to be able to anticipate things and think about the future. Imagining possibilities was something embedded in the structure of the philosophical curriculum in Wallenstein's time. Being able to distinguish between what was likely to occur and what was not required hard work. The general had to collect a lot of information, yet he drew different conclusions than his enemies did. He brooded over his decisions so long that his own allies charged him with being indecisive. Nevertheless, all he did was refrain from rushing to judgment.

You can weigh options, however, only once you have settled on a certain framework and strategies for judging your options. Wallenstein, a choleric person himself, was a master at getting under the skin of his enemies and predicting their every move. He "became" the enemy. Such thinking, however, takes time and energy. Leadership success depends on how you weigh your information, your options, and your ability to resist making rash decisions. Finally, a leader has to be somewhat secretive and careful about whom she trusts.

All the abilities I have mentioned so far are not yet virtues (and Wallenstein was the opposite of what I would call virtuous), but they come to their full fruition in a person who is also moral.[1]

Ubuntu as a Key to Moral Leadership

Leaders are the heads of certain groups. They are successful if they can motivate their group members toward a common goal. But if, because of their own virtues, they are also able to inspire moral behavior in others and create a genuine harmony within the group, then they are real achievers. Such *ethical leadership* is centered on dealing with others in a positive, moral way.

African philosophy has carved out a wonderful example: *Ubuntu*. It embodies the predominant, traditionally African approach to society, focused on care, community, harmony, hospitality, respect, and responsiveness. Applied to modern contexts, *ubuntu* means that a leader has to build strong relationships by affirming everyone's personhood. The contemporary world contains countless examples of dehumanization. If you use social media, chances are that you will often find posts that deny someone's membership in the human family or society, negate their right to exist or think for themselves, or even wish the other person dead. *Ubuntu* encourages *ungumuntu*, which means "he or she is a person too."[2]

Philosophy helps us to see that we are all connected by the powers of reasoning, remembering, imagining, and willing; we all desire joy and fulfillment, whether we are African or European. The use of reason helps us to dispel the myths of racial superiority and cut through the fog of racist prejudice.

Ubuntu is a way of establishing harmony in a diverse culture. If our political leaders would take it seriously, they would have to begin to transform their own hearts and minds accordingly. They would have to become moral by being *with* the community, by caring for it, and especially by stopping the radicalized bias and hatred toward those who think differently.

Ubuntu is not so different from traditional Christian worldviews and political philosophies of the common good. The main problem today, however, is identifying *what* this good should be. In the West, we have replaced the good of the whole society with goods for certain voter groups, politicians, and the lobbies they serve. These goods are not universal, are often in conflict with each other, and eliminate the possibility of a just society because everybody is out to serve *only* his own constituents.

Can we even establish a *shared vision* of society for all? A true leader would start conversations about commonly held beliefs and values and would work to create an atmosphere in which everyone can be a *person* and be heard if she or he wants to speak.

Leadership requires good judgment, and that comes through reflection. What does that mean? A leader not only has to think about others but also has to *know herself*. Philosophers of many different persuasions have written about this journey into the self, perhaps most famously St. Augustine, a fourth-century thinker.[3]

By reflecting on myself, I make the self an object; it is a bit like taking a step outside my body and looking at it. Part of this self-exploration is called self-awareness. How do I come across to others? What do people think of me and my actions? And so forth. Yet philosophical self-exploration goes much further. It explores the depths of the human heart and mind. Why do I do the things I do? Why do I believe certain things? Have I learned from my experiences or do I refuse to do so?

Asking these and many other questions might bring us some uncertainty because we will not find easy answers, but this *uncertainty* should keep us honest. We do not have all the answers, and we may not be able to understand ourselves completely. Thus reflection makes us more human and invites us to broaden our perspectives. It helps us mature in ethical reasoning and also moral behavior.

A leader must be able to reflect on herself and the world in order to make good judgments and consider other viewpoints; otherwise, she might consider herself invincible and fall into ruin. An excellent tool for reflection is the practice of keeping a journal. I keep one for personal growth and one for research ideas that pop into my head. By going over my notes, I am able to chart my progress and see where I need to improve. As with every other philosophical exercise, the key is to make reflection a constant part of your life and to do it often, so that it becomes more effective.[4]

Recognizing and Hearing the Other

One of the most common complaints people make about their workplace is that they don't feel appreciated. Much of what people mean by *appreciation* falls under respect for the person, as *ubuntu* describes it. For instance, a worker at a Ford factory once had the chance to tell his company CEO, "I used to hate coming to work here. But lately I have been asked what I think, and that makes me feel like I'm somebody. I never thought the company would see me as a human being. Now I like coming to work."[5]

Perhaps the most successful "CEO" of all times was Benedict of Nursia. He lived in the fifth century, and his rules for running a community have been observed in countless communities ever since. The "rules" he wrote down were for religious communities, such as Benedictine monasteries, but they are full of wisdom. For example, important decisions were discussed in meetings, and all monks were admonished not to ignore the voice of the youngest and most immature members, because even theirs might contain wisdom![6]

Philosophy takes ordinary reflection to a deeper level: it requires me to step out of myself and begin to recognize the other in order to tame my selfishness and become moral. I must freely make the choice to end my self-centeredness and pay attention to the other because it is only through others and my interaction with them that I begin to *know myself*. I only get to know others if I *never* treat them as means to an end. Such a philosophy of recognition can have many forms and be based on different premises.[7]

Although there are many more aspects of leadership, I only want to focus on one more: *perseverance*. Leaders do not quit unless their survival or the good of their group requires it. Nevertheless, this brings up something that many people do not think much about—namely, the ability to deal with tension and *conflict*. I have an acquaintance who always finds excuses for the most immature behavior of his adult children, usually laughing it off. He has always avoided conflict and could never stand up to his children, telling them how badly they were behaving. It's not our place here to ask why this person acts this way but rather what it means *philo-sophically*. If you are able to stomach conflict and thrive in spite of it, you can be a leader who is not pushed around by emotions or others, thereby endangering the group. You have to be able to stand your ground.

The basis for perseverance or endurance is *fortitude*. It means not engaging in perilous behavior but instead having the wisdom to decide when to risk something for a greater good, when to stand firm, and when to withdraw. It instills in you the strength to hold on to the good even in a time of adversity, even in great conflict, and thus it allows you to persevere. Fortitude or courage, however, is based on another virtue—namely, wisdom, which allows me to *discern* what is worth taking a risk for. Without wisdom there is no proper assessment of risk, and it is wisdom that counsels against rash decisions or listening to irrational and extreme voices.[8]

17

Creative Thinking Is Not a Mystery

"T
alent hits a target no one else can hit. Genius hits a target no one else can see."[1] This is how the German philosopher Arthur Schopenhauer summed up his thinking about who a genius is. Now, most of us never daydream about being a genius, but I bet that many of us wonder why we are not more successful in what we do: Why can't we be more creative and come up with new and exciting ideas? Why can't I be just a little bit like a genius?

Many people talk about creativity and creative thinking but rarely give a definition of what that actually means. The word *creative* comes from the Latin verb *creare*, meaning to bring into existence. Whatever is brought into existence is *new*, so creative thinking could mean the production of new ideas or, as others have called it, *original thinking*.[2] The nineteenth-century German philosopher Hermann von Helmholtz was one of the first to be interested in the problem of creativity. He saw that it was linked to *saturation*, which is the process in which one gathers facts and the raw material for the production of new ideas. Then it was connected to an *incubation* period, when the mind sorts through this material and lets it sink to the bottom of the subconscious. It is what I describe as "going pregnant with an idea," which means carrying it around in your heart and mind until you are able to put your finger on it. Once that occurs, you have the flash of insight needed for phase three, the *illumination*.[3]

Since then, many psychologists, sociologists, and philosophers have tried to improve Helmholtz's observations. One of the most helpful approaches I have found is describing creativity as the combination of several different thought processes—namely, convergent, divergent, and lateral thinking.

Divergence, Convergence, and Lateral Thinking

Divergent thinking means exploring ideas in a number of different ways. Imagine a dot on a piece of paper from which arrows emanate in all directions, with each arrow symbolizing an idea or choice to pursue. In divergent thinking, we try to combine patterns and solutions we found before and test them in our mind. Are they coherent, do they make sense, do they actually belong together? We are focusing on a problem. Consequently, a necessary condition for divergent thinking is *openness*. It does not mean "keeping an open mind" but instead has to do with the miracle that the human mind is open to all of reality and can focus its attention wherever it wants. Such openness differentiates us from animals, who have a much narrower field of intention. An example of divergent thinking is the art of *reduction* in philosophy. We take a concept and split it up into its elements. These elements can be different from, similar to, or identical with other elements in the world. As we compare and combine these elements in a logical fashion, new concepts and new ideas come into existence. Divergent thinking is, in my opinion, much more than *brainstorming* because we have to make judgments and ask evaluative questions. Divergent thinking alone, however, would leave us in a labyrinth of thoughts. It easily loses sight of what is important. *Convergent* thinking, however, helps us regain clarity and can be compared to a glass lens that bundles many light rays into one spot.

Convergence, however, presupposes good judgment and logic. You have to be able to think precisely and know how to combine subjects and predicates. "America is a democracy" is a true statement, but in order to make it, you have to know what democracy means and what America is. Convergent thinking forces us to be methodical and to have a certain way of proceeding (see the remarks on method in chap. 7). *Disputative thinking* is a kind of divergent thinking because it allows us to consider other paths and double check our solutions by imagining and then disputing the best arguments against our claims or solutions.

Lateral thinking is primarily about trying to look at the same problem from all kinds of angles and viewpoints. It is the opposite of *linear* thinking, where you have only one viewpoint or perspective. For example, let's say you have a coin in front of you. You can look at it based on how valuable it is—in this case, it is worth two hundred dollars. You could, however, also look at it from a historical perspective to determine where and when it was produced. You could even investigate its exact metallic composition, such as how much copper or other elements are mixed in with the silver.

All three thinking processes play an important role in what the ancient philosophers called the *ars inveniendi*, or the art of inventing, which is just as useful in making arguments in a speech as it is in finding a solution to a problem. All three presuppose that you are able to imagine possibilities, which brings us back to the concept of openness: the person who is willing to open the boxes of settled meanings and concepts can combine them and bring into existence something that was not there before.[4]

I use the *ars inveniendi* frequently in my research but also when I mentor graduate students. I often compare writing a good master's thesis or dissertation with fishing because I think it can provide a roadmap for convergent thinking. First, you have to decide where to fish. There are countless lakes, just as there are innumerable topics to write on. Then you have to ask yourself what kind of fish you want to catch or what kind of dissertation you want to write.

If you can't name the fish, you won't have the right hook or bait, and if you cannot clearly express the concept or the idea you are chasing, you had better stay off the lake. These are all important, practical things to consider, and honest reflection will help you know whether the topic or problem is one you can tackle.

Overcoming Mental Blocks

All three thinking processes also help you to see the right problem and separate it from things that are not important. John Arnold has argued that many people lack the ability to *isolate a problem*. They have either mental, social, or cultural blocks that inhibit them. These people get hung up on surface issues.[5] Here philosophy can be of great assistance. By using philosophical categories, one can peel away the layers from a problem and identify necessary and unnecessary connections.

Many years ago, I was invited to interview for a position as associate dean of a graduate school. During the interview, the dean told me that the biggest problem they had was the falling retention rate of students. Too many never finished their degree or finished it below grade expectations. When he asked me what I would change to make things better, I told him, "I would train every graduate student, before they even begin school, in time management. That is the key to retention." My solution was different than what he expected because neither he nor his employees had isolated this problem. Many graduate students do not know how to structure their lives or how to balance their private and university lives, and thus they are more likely to drop out, leaving with a feeling of frustration and inadequacy. Instead of getting to the real problem, the dean and his employees only saw the dropping retention rate and thought they could address it by increasing funding or adjusting the program. A few months after my interview, the university initiated time management programs for graduate students but did not give me the job. In hindsight, that was a blessing.

How to Become Creative

A year or so ago, one of my daughters came home from school sobbing because she had received a bad grade on a writing assignment. "I am so bad at this," she cried. "I am just not creative!" This was not really the case, though. One part of the problem was that she lacked proper instruction. Until that point, our daughter had been attending a bilingual school, and since she was dedicating so much time to learning a foreign language, she had never learned how to write fiction. The other problem was her *self-perception*. I reminded her of the many art projects she had completed over the summer, her knitting and sewing projects, how she had invented new games and activities for her younger siblings, and many other things. "Don't you think all these things were very creative?" After thinking about it from a different perspective, she could see that maybe she was more creative than she thought.

Most of the time, we do not *think of ourselves as creative*, and that is the biggest stumbling block to real creativity. You might be able to solve some problems really well, but when it comes to bigger problems, you will fail because you block yourself from the inside. For me, some of the most entertaining moments on television are when people in reality-TV shows have to come up with "bush fixes," such as constructing a geothermal heating system out of a few old plastic barrels and hoses, or molding a sophisticated machine part out of scrap metal. I doubt that any of these people would call themselves creative, but most people would dare say that they are. Perhaps they do not identify as creative because they fear the pressure of being "ingenious" all the time, but no one is always in top form. Creative thinking is a way of approaching the world, nothing more.[6]

Self-perception is crucial for successful creativity. The phrase "Know thyself" has always been emphasized in philosophy since its beginnings in ancient Greece. We should get to know our abilities and limitations. Some of us are lucky enough to grow up in circumstances that foster such curiosity and creativity, but young minds are often starved by being exposed to too many digital influences.

As a person with ADHD, I constantly ask questions. It took my wife a long time to understand this, and I still sometimes drive her crazy. I cannot stop asking questions about why this or that exists or has to be done in a certain way, and I am happy that my teachers always encouraged me to keep asking, even though I often tired them out too.

All of the thinking patterns I have outlined above exist in some kind of mixed form and rely on *challenging the status quo* by questioning why something has always been done a certain way. Challenging such conventional views is usually called "thinking outside the box." Bureaucrats in particular love conventions and following rules. As a teacher, I sometimes find this tiresome because I can often think of better ways to address a problem. If I had a dollar for every time I've had to attend a two-hour meeting for a problem that could have been solved in ten minutes via email, I would be rich. The same goes for inviting every staff member to a meeting that only requires a handful of key people. Was it ever asked whether this was actually a good use of time and resources, or did superiors just rely on outdated models of leadership?

Apart from addressing old problems by challenging traditional approaches, *new problems* cry out for novel solutions. If we use conventional means for addressing them, we set ourselves up for likely failure. The important question is, How do I answer such a challenge?

The best way to approach a new problem is to define it carefully. Definitions are probably the most hated philosophical tool. They are used to describe the *essence* of something or its necessary characteristics.[7] A door, for instance, is "a flat object that is used to close the entrance of something such as a room or building, or the entrance itself," according to the *Cambridge Dictionary*.[8] We can challenge this definition by taking it apart and trying to redefine it, going through each element and replacing it with another. Redefining a concept is hard work, though, and it takes time and discipline.

So you see, philosophy is not impractical but gives us a structure through which we can develop new ideas that are logical, coherent, and creative.[9]

18

Reasoning Helps Us Find Unity in a Divided World

As a foreigner, I have always been fascinated by the American motto *E pluribus unum*, yet I never understood it as a factual statement. After all, we all know how divided this country is and how communities are often racially, economically, and politically separated. Nevertheless, the American motto expresses a normative expectation of unity. It hopes that people of different backgrounds and creeds can somehow bring about a familial unity. This moral vision of a unified country can benefit from the insights of philosophy.

In chapter 4, we saw that we all are individual beings (*principle of identity*). Every one of us is indivisible and thus an *individuum*. Each and every one of us is a unity in herself, a closed unit that does not need anything else to be added to it or subtracted from it. In *that* sense, each individual is perfect.

Isn't it ironic, then, that even though each of us is a *center of unity*, it is so hard to achieve *unity among individuals*? After all, we share all these characteristics and still cannot live in harmony. But of course each of us also has free will and therefore his or her own ideas, and thus creating unity is a bit like bringing myriad separate universes together under one hat. Some even wonder

157

whether unity among humans is even possible. What would it look like?

We know from observing nature that many individual animals can work together in a hive or a group. What unites them are common goals such as providing for food and shelter, a plan for survival. By accepting such an overarching *plan*, they begin to form a unity, a new whole. What could such a plan look like for humans? What could motivate us to unity? Can the values of a constitution be the frame for such unity, and if so, would that not demand a similarly deep appreciation of these values by all who engage in this new unity? Or are more pragmatic motivations needed, such as protection of life and survival?

As interesting as these questions may be, I doubt their answers will entice unity in this society because they always presuppose too much, either in shared values and politics, or religion, or even the view of the human person. Perhaps a more humble and basic approach based on philosophy alone can help.

Such an approach would ask, first of all: *What kind of unity are we aspiring to?* That is a tough question, but we can try answering it by looking at ourselves. Each and every individual constitutes unity. Each is one and consequently not the other. The fact that I exist means I am different from another. I am a whole being, and my soul unites all aspects of who I am. I am a bit like a perfect sphere in geometry; nothing must be added or subtracted to make me "me." An individual could therefore claim "I am unity" and experience in this regard perfection.

Consequently, I would think, a group that wants to integrate me *must allow me to live a similar experience of perfection.* It must enable, to put it in different words, the integral fulfillment of the whole human person, physically and spiritually (see the discussion on natural law in chap. 13). Yet no bigger unity such as a society can convincingly draw us into unified action if it is not based on *goodness*, and it will not convince us of its goodness if it is not *truthful.* Only goodness and truth can inspire hope, a hope that I can trust that this society cherishes me and my fulfillment, cares for me, and wishes me well.

What hope really means became clear to me when I was twenty-two and my mother was dying of cancer. I had never prayed like I did then, and I hoped for a cure. It didn't come, and the year after her death, burdened with insomnia, grief, and anger, was gut-wrenching. I began to read books on existential philosophy and death but also on the human person. I realized that many of my hopes were just egotistical wishes. So much in my life was about me and me alone. That was a painful but a life-changing discovery.

I began to force myself to pay attention to every face I encountered because I could not remember my mother's very well. I had taken it for granted that she would always be there. I did not want to go through that again with anyone. I did not want to fall again into the pit of being caught up in myself and disconnected from others. Hope was not something just internal to me but was ingrained in human relationships, I realized. It meant more than expecting a brighter future. Hope never comes just for me *alone*; it only comes if I pass it on to others, if I elicit hope and joy in others.

Thus, on a societal level we should not expect unity if we cannot give each other hope. Yet for that to happen everybody has to be a cherished part of the community.

Connectedness and Personhood

Let me give you an example. My classes are in a big building with seventy-five lecture halls and seminar rooms. Two women are responsible for cleaning the entire building, plus shoveling snow in the winter. They are always hard at work, cleaning the bathrooms, emptying the trash cans, and picking up the paper cups students leave behind, but hardly anyone acknowledges them. Whenever I see these women, I greet them and ask them how they are doing, and often we chat for a few minutes. Their faces light up every time because someone took the time to get to know them. I dare to think I give them a glimmer of hope, and they give me hope because I encounter goodness and truth in them.

Many of the stories I have heard from these women have had a greater impact on me than what some of my smartest colleagues have said, because nothing is weightier than a profound encounter with another person. These types of encounters give me hope. They exemplify for me that there is something fundamentally good in humanity, but they also remind me that this good cannot flourish to the fullest extent because of a number of factors—and I might be one of them.

It was philosophical reflection on what a person is—namely, a "thou" and never a thing—that made me pay better attention to others. All humans have common needs, such as the need to be recognized, listened to, and appreciated, and we all have an undeniable dignity. What would happen if more people engaged in such thinking, humbly listening to each other in an effort to understand and appreciate our differences but also our unity in the human family?

Profound encounters bring about connectedness. Often you hear the slogan "We are all in this together," but it only captures a small part of connectedness. It only pertains to a certain event or thing, such as a global pandemic or a recession. The type of connectedness that I have in mind goes deeper than this. I grasped this when I wrote my doctoral dissertation in philosophy. Christian Wolff, a German philosopher of the eighteenth century, made the "nexus of everything" the foundation of his thought. Everything, he taught, was interconnected in a great chain of being.[1] I knew, of course, about ecosystems and our place in them and so forth, but for the first time it occurred to me that *my* connection with everything was deeper than I thought. I was made out of carbon like the tree in my front yard; I was just as mortal as the spider I crushed under my foot and my soul was just as immaterial as a number. I was connected to all that exists and somehow participated in this theater of the universe.

But why was I connected, and what was the meaning of all this? Seeing connections makes you see commonalities or bridges that you didn't see before. It makes you put experiences into a bigger context, letting you see the *whole* that you neglected before. How was I complicit in destroying the environment? How could I help? Was I not contributing to the problem of exploiting part-time professors by getting benefits such as sabbaticals?

Connectedness is a hotly discussed topic in a number of professions such as health care, but it should really be of concern for *all* of us. If we take the insight about connectedness seriously, then it should bother us when other people are treated badly and do not have the same opportunities we have. It helps us realize the responsibilities we have as social animals. Connectedness creates a "home," and we have to ask ourselves whom we shut out or deny a place in it.[2]

Giving All a "Home"

We all need a "spiritual" home, as Tom V. Morris calls it, which is much more than the roof above our head.[3] We need a community in which we acknowledge a deep and active sense of commitment and where we also feel protected, accepted, and appreciated. It is part of our identity.

However, many in the United States feel they are no longer part of the "American Dream" or never were, or they feel otherwise excluded. Some groups fear that their individuality would be threatened if they became part of a "home." Philosophical reflection can not only make us attentive to such needs but also help us to demonstrate that there are different levels of identity.

A sense of unity does not mean giving up the boundaries that liberty, enshrined in the Constitution, provides. In fact, an analysis of unity and community can show us that it is the *boundaries* we create around us that bring about society and create free spaces for us.[4]

There is no unity without those free centers of action we call persons. In a politically and culturally divisive world, it has become impossible to identify specific goods we all agree on; the idea of the common good is often invoked, but the reality of it is long dead. Yet are there no other ways of creating community? Again, if we put on our philosopher's hat, we might be able to find some ways toward the establishment of community.

Instead of just looking to specific goods, such as certain kinds of legislation (e.g., universal health care), we could try to foster in our communities an appreciation of the unique dignity of every person, a sense of solidarity with those in need and distress, and especially protection for all. Without feeling safe, you cannot prosper or even begin to think about the greater unity of the country and the human family!

Part of experiencing a "home" means that there are *rituals and symbols* you can identify with. Yet what should we do with symbols that are ambiguous or offend others? The philosopher will point to the power of memory. It plays a crucial part in making us who we are. Creating spaces of *collective memory* and reworking others so that more social groups can attach a positive symbolic meaning to them will be of importance for unity in a society.

Listening to others humbly and compassionately is the first step toward creating community and acknowledging each other's place in the same "home."[5]

Unity in Diversity

"There are many rooms in my Father's house" (John 14:2) is one of the most beautiful passages in the entire Bible. It shows us that even in heaven there is diversity. Celebrating diversity has become a cultural value, but most often it only refers to increasing the number of various types of minorities in a business or organization. While this is crucially important, we most often forget the *diversity of opinions*. In fact, a diversity of opinions is often no longer desired in our world.

More often than we might realize, we deny a place in the "home" of our communities to those with whom we profoundly disagree. This is understandable and ethical if they directly endanger us, but let us assume that there are more people of goodwill than not. What do disagreements about cherished beliefs between such people look like in our country? Most often, they quickly become emotional and personal. Moral values are undermined—in short, we do everything *but* "dispute" our differences with the powers of reason.

Even more disappointing is that we habitually make our opponent's arguments weaker than they actually are by ridiculing or distorting them. From Thomas Aquinas I learned that in the days of medieval philosophy, the philosopher's rule was the exact opposite. Philosophers lived according to the principle: *Always make your opponent's argument as strong as possible.* That's probably what I found most fascinating about the scholastic tradition of philosophy. The Scholastics valued diversity of opinion, which did not mean that they did not have clear convictions about which opinions were wrong. Yet they tried to understand opposing viewpoints, even if only to refute them. Theirs was a real fight for truth, not a yelling match.

In the US, two contemporaries come to mind—scholars and intellectuals who embody the honest search for truth, despite disagreeing about many things: Cornel West and Robert P. George. West, who until recently taught at Harvard, is honorary cochair of the Democratic Socialists of America and an outspoken proponent of programs and policies traditionally associated with the left side of the political spectrum. George, who teaches at Princeton, is a conservative who is equally outspoken in criticizing left-leaning programs and policies and advocating ideas associated with the right side of the divide. Countless times they have appeared on stage together, yet what impressed participants and viewers of their debates was not so much their arguments but the way they listened to each other. Not only do they address each other as "brother," but they actually mean it. They are close, personal friends.

Such friendships have become rare today because they demand the humility to listen to someone you think is wrong but who is nevertheless a unique person with infinite value and dignity—and who therefore might have something profound to say. In 2017, they published a statement together that is a more fitting conclusion to this book than anything I could ever write:

> None of us is infallible. Whether you are a person of the left, the right, or the center, there are reasonable people of goodwill who do not share your fundamental convictions. . . .
>
> All of us should be willing—even eager—to engage with anyone who is prepared to do business in the currency of truth-seeking discourse by offering reasons, marshaling evidence, and making arguments. The more important the subject under discussion, the more willing we should be to listen and engage—especially if the person with whom we are in conversation will challenge our deeply held—even our most cherished and identity-forming—beliefs. . . .
>
> Our willingness to listen to and respectfully engage those with whom we disagree (especially about matters of profound importance) contributes vitally to the maintenance of a milieu in which people feel free to speak their minds, consider unpopular positions, and explore lines of argument that may undercut established ways of thinking. Such an ethos protects us against dogmatism and groupthink, both of which are toxic to the health of academic communities and to the functioning of democracies.[6]

Notes

Introduction

1. Marcus Aurelius, *Ad Se Ipsum*, book 4, n. 3, ed. Jan Hendrik Leopold (Leipzig: Teubner, 1908), Perseus Digital Library, www.perseus.tufts.edu. The Greek word in question is ὑπόληψις.

2. Von Braun had been a Nazi scientist, who was offered—despite his past—a new life in the US, developing its space program along with other former Nazi scientists. See Wayne Biddle, *Dark Side of the Moon: Wernher von Braun, the Third Reich and the Space Race* (New York: Norton, 2009).

3. "Partisan Antipathy: More Intense, More Personal," Pew Research Center, October 10, 2019, https://www.people-press.org/2019/10/10/partisan-antipathy -more-intense-more-personal; Levi Boxell, Matthew Gentzkow, and Jesse M. Shapiro, "Cross-Country Trends in Affective Polarization," June 2020, https:// www.brown.edu/Research/Shapiro/pdfs/cross-polar.pdf.

4. Zaid Jilani and Jeremy Adam Smith, "What Is the True Cost of Polarization in America?," *Greater Good Magazine*, March 4, 2019, https://greatergood.berkeley .edu/article/item/what_is_the_true_cost_of_polarization_in_america; Samara Klar, Yanna Krupnikov, and John Barry Ryan, "Is America Hopelessly Polarized, or Just Allergic to Politics?," opinion, *New York Times*, April 12, 2019, https:// www.nytimes.com/2019/04/12/opinion/polarization-politics-democrats-repub licans.html; Frank Newport, "The Impact of Increased Political Polarization," Gallup, December 5, 2019, https://news.gallup.com/opinion/polling-matters /268982/impact-increased-political-polarization.aspx; John Avlon, "Polariza- tion Is Poisoning America. Here's an Antidote," opinion, CNN, November 1, 2019, https://edition.cnn.com/2019/10/30/opinions/fractured-states-of-america -polarization-is-killing-us-avlon/index.html.

Chapter 1: Knowledge Is the Basis of Good Reasoning

1. Aristotle, *Physics* 194 b17–20; see also his *Posterior Analytics* 71 b9–11; 94 a20.

2. This chapter is based on the work of August Brunner, *Erkenntnistheorie* (Kolmar: Alsatia, 1949), 1–51. A fascinating new approach, with some commonalities to the one laid out here, is developed by Charles Taylor, *The Language Animal: The Full Shape of the Human Linguistic Capacity* (Cambridge, MA: Harvard University Press, 2016).

3. Brunner, *Erkenntnistheorie*, 28. Helpful for our problem is also Roger Scruton, *On Human Nature* (Princeton: Princeton University Press, 2017), 50–78.

4. Brunner, *Erkenntnistheorie*, 29. For an exposition of openness as a characteristic of the human mind, I do not know of any English book rivaling Walter Hoeres, *Offenheit und Distanz: Grundzüge einer phänomenologischen Anthropologie* (Berlin: Duncker & Humblot, 1993).

5. Brunner, *Erkenntnistheorie*, 32.

6. James Warren, *The Pleasures of Reason in Plato, Aristotle, and the Hellenistic Hedonists* (Cambridge: Cambridge University Press, 2014), 157–74; Mette Lebach, "The Recognition of Human Dignity in the Person Living with Dementia," in *Irish Reader in Moral Theology: The Legacy of the Last Fifty Years*, vol. 3, *Medical and Bio Ethics*, ed. Enda McDonagh and Vincent MacNamara (Dublin: Columba, 2013), 66–76.

7. Immanuel Kant, *Metaphysik der Sitten: Metaphysische Anfangsgründe der Tugendlehre* [*Metaphysics of Morals: The Doctrine of Virtue*] (Berlin: Academy of Sciences, 1907), AA 6:399, 401, 411f.

8. Thomas Buchheim, *Aristoteles* (Freiburg: Herder, 1999), 150; Immanuel Kant, *Metaphysik der Sitten*, AA 6:484–85; Theres Lehn, "Asketische Praxis: Die Bedeutung der Askese für das ethische Handeln und das menschliche Sein bei Aristoteles und Michel de Foucault" (PhD thesis, Ludwig Maximilian University, Munich, 2012); cf. Albert Auer, *Die philosophischen Grundlagen der Askese* (Salzburg: Jgonta, 1946).

9. Max Scheler, *Man's Place in Nature*, trans. Hans Meyerhoff (New York: Beacon, 1961), 37.

10. Hans-Eduard Hengstenberg, "La decision initiale et les structures des activites humaines," *Revue de Metaphysique et de Morale* 3 (1972): 286–306; Andrew Michel Flescher, *Heroes, Saints, and Ordinary Morality* (Washington, DC: Georgetown University Press, 2003), 174–78.

Chapter 2: Have Realistic Goals and Humility

1. See Plato, *Apology* 21c–d; *Charmides* 165b, 166c. See also Gail Fine, "Does Socrates Claim to Know That He Knows Nothing?," *Oxford Studies in Ancient Philosophy* 35 (2008): 49–88, which explains the background of the saying and its philosophical significance.

2. See Kurt Pritzl, ed., *Truth: Studies of a Robust Presence* (Washington, DC: Catholic University of America Press, 2010); Thomas Gloeckner, *Über Wahrheit, oder Der Grund der Suche nach Wahrheit* (Munich: AVM, 2012); Jennifer Nagel, *Knowledge: A Very Short Introduction* (Oxford: Oxford University Press, 2014).

3. John Kruger and David Dunning, "Unskilled and Unaware of It: How Difficulties in Recognizing One's Own Incompetence Lead to Inflated Self-Assessments,"

Journal of Personality and Social Psychology 77, no. 6 (1999): 1121–34; David Dunning, "The Dunning-Kruger Effect: On Being Ignorant of One's Own Ignorance," *Advances in Experimental Social Psychology* 44 (2011): 247–96; Gordon Pennycook, Robert M. Ross, Derek J. Koehler, and Jonathan A. Fugelsang, "Dunning-Kruger Effects in Reasoning: Theoretical Implications of the Failure to Recognize Incompetence," *Psychonomic Bulletin Review* 24, no. 6 (December 2017): 1774–84, https://doi.org/10.3758/s13423-017-1242-7.

4. A good introduction to the philosophy of personalism, which emphasizes the uniqueness and value of the human person, is Juan Manuel Burgos, *An Introduction to Personalism* (Washington, DC: Catholic University of America Press, 2018).

5. Robert Spaemann, *Persons: The Difference between Someone and Something* (Oxford: Oxford University Press, 2017); Harald Schöndorf, *Erkenntnistheorie* (Stuttgart: Kohlhammer, 2014), 140–45.

Chapter 3: The Power of Reason and Eternity

1. Joseph Flanagan, *The Quest for Knowledge: An Essay in Lonergan's Philosophy* (Toronto: University of Toronto Press, 1997), 56.

2. Joseph Bochenski, *Wege zum philosophischen Denken* (Freiburg: Herder, 1959), 11–22 (author's translation).

Chapter 4: Knowing Yourself Is the Key to Logical Thinking

1. Jean-Paul Richter, cited by Jacques Maritain, *A Preface to Metaphysics* (New York: Sheed & Ward, 1947), 47.

2. Cicero, *De officiis* 1.32 (author's translation).

3. Maritain, *Preface to Metaphysics*, 94.

4. Aristotle, *De anima* 3.5.

5. In my view, the best text on human dependency is Alasdair MacIntyre, *Dependent Rational Animals: Why Human Beings Need the Virtues* (Chicago: Open Court, 1999).

6. Hans-Eduard Hengstenberg, *Philosophische Anthropologie*, 4th ed. (Stuttgart: Kohlhammer, 1984); Winfried Weier, *Strukturen menschlicher Existenz: Grenzen heutigen Philosophierens* (Paderborn: Schöningh, 1977); Weier, *Brennpunkte der Gegenwartsphilosophie: Zentralthemen und Tendenzen im Zeitalter des Nihilismus* (Darmstadt: WBG, 1991).

Chapter 5: Good Thinking Is Always Focused

1. For a discussion of this, see Edward Feser, *Philosophy of Mind* (Oxford: Oneworld, 2005).

2. I use a hyphen here to indicate that *state-ment* is different from the regular *statement*. *State-ment* means that we perceive a certain state of affairs on a thing, while *statement* can be any sentence we utter.

3. See Martin Honecker, *Das Denken* (Berlin: Dümmler, 1935), 18.

4. Therese Scarpelli Cory, "Aquinas on the Agent Intellect's Causation of the Intelligible," *Recherchés de théologie et philosophie médiévales* 82 (2015): 1–60; James S. Kintz, "The Illuminative Function of the Agent Intellect," *British Journal for the History of Philosophy* 27 (2019): 3–22. For the enterprise of philosophy as a search for intelligible forms, see the brilliant essay by Joseph Geyser, *Eidologie, oder Philosophie als Formerkenntis* (Freiburg: Herder, 1920). For a general overview of Aquinas's theory of cognition, see Adam Wood, *Aquinas and the Immateriality of the Human Mind* (Washington, DC: Catholic University of America Press, 2020), 152–92.

5. See the discussion of forms in Mortimer J. Adler, *Aristotle for Everybody: Difficult Thought Made Easy* (New York: Simon & Schuster, 1978).

6. See, e.g., John Haldane, "Aquinas and the Active Intellect," *Philosophy* 67 (1992): 199–210.

7. For a general overview of the philosophical problems of postmodernism, see Richard Bailey, "Overcoming Veriphobia—Learning to Love Truth Again," *British Journal of Educational Studies* 49 (2001): 159–72; Norman Levitt and Paul Gross, *Higher Superstition: The Academic Left and Its Quarrels with Science* (Baltimore: Johns Hopkins University Press, 1997), 71–106; J. P. Moreland and William L. Craig, *Philosophical Foundations for a Christian Worldview* (Downers Grove, IL: InterVarsity, 2003), 130–53; Armin Kreiner, *Ende der Wahrheit? Zum Wahrheitsverständnis in Philosophie und Theologie* (Freiburg: Herder, 1991).

8. Aristotle, *Topica* 1. For a detailed discussion of the predicables, see Peter Coffey, *The Science of Logic: An Inquiry into the Principles of Accurate Thought and Scientific Method* (London: Longmans, 1912), 1:72–88.

9. For a detailed discussion, see Coffey, *Science of Logic*, 1:154–291.

10. On truth claims in judgments, see Joseph Geyser, *Grundlagen der Logik und Erkenntnislehre* (Munster: Schöningh, 1909), 73; Celestine Bittle, *The Science of Correct Thinking* (Milwaukee: Bruce, 1950), 102.

11. For an excellent overview of syllogisms and fallacies, see Peter Kreeft, *Socratic Logic* (South Bend, IN: St. Augustine's Press, 2010), 215–312.

12. Of the many fun and readable books about fallacies and mistakes in reasoning, the best are Nathaniel Bluedorn and Hans Bluedorn, *The Fallacy Detective: Thirty-Eight Lessons on How to Recognize Bad Reasoning*, 4th ed. (Muscatine, IA: Christian Logic, 2015); and Nathaniel Bluedorn and Hans Bluedorn, *The Thinking Toolbox* (Muscatine, IA: Christian Logic, 2005).

13. There are many good logic books, but I still prefer Bittle, *Science of Correct Thinking*; Kreeft, *Socratic Logic*; and Peter Smith, *Introduction to Formal Logic* (Cambridge: Cambridge University Press, 2003).

14. On categories, see Kreeft, *Socratic Logic*, 54–56; Coffey, *Science of Logic*, 1:135–53. For a first overview, see Celestine Bittle, *The Domain of Being: Ontology* (Milwaukee: Bruce, 1939), 211–39.

15. For the question of analogy of being, see Thomas J. White, ed., *The Analogy of Being: Invention of the Antichrist or Wisdom of God?* (Grand Rapids: Eerdmans, 2010). A good introduction to philosophical theology is still Tom V.

Morris, *Our Idea of God: An Introduction to Philosophical Theology* (Vancouver: Regent, 1991).

16. See, e.g., Janet Martin Soskice, *The Kindness of God: Metaphor, Gender, and Religious Language* (Oxford: Oxford University Press, 2007).

17. A good reader on the topic is Richard Swinburne, ed., *The Justification of Induction* (Oxford: Oxford University Press, 1974); cf. Alister E. McGrath, *The Territories of Human Reason: Science and Theology in an Age of Multiple Rationalities* (Oxford: Oxford University Press, 2019), 155–82.

Chapter 6: Critical Thinking

1. Peter Nardi, *Critical Thinking: Tools for Evaluating Research* (Berkeley: University of California Press, 2017), 2–45.

2. If one does not believe in truth, one cannot be critical. For the most recent defense of the classical correspondence theory of truth, which I present throughout this book, see Joshua Rasmussen, *Defending the Correspondence Theory of Truth* (Cambridge: Cambridge University Press, 2014).

3. I find the parallel to love quite intriguing. Erich Fromm shows that love is an art but that most people neglect to put it first in their lives and desire it with perseverance. See Fromm, *The Art of Loving* (New York: Harper Perennial, 2006).

4. See Norbert Michel, John James Carter III, and Otmar Varela, "Active versus Passive Teaching Styles: An Empirical Study of Student Learning Outcomes," *Human Resource Quarterly* 20 (2009): 397–418.

5. Ulrich L. Lehner, *Enlightened Monks: The German Benedictines, 1740–1803* (Oxford: Oxford University Press, 2010); on the problems of interpreting visuals, see Nardi, *Critical Thinking*, 64–91; on critical scientific thinking and distinguishing science from pseudoscience, see Nardi, *Critical Thinking*, 106–26.

6. Every student should read the short but brilliant essay by Carl Sagan, "The Fine Art of Baloney Detection," which can be found on many websites. Sometimes it is merely called the "Baloney Detection Kit." A good introduction to dealing with scientific data and their abuse is Carl Bergstrom and Jevin West, *Calling Bullshit: The Art of Skepticism in a Data-Driven World* (New York: Random House, 2020).

7. An excellent resource, especially for high schoolers, is the wonderful textbook by my colleague Christopher Baglow, *Faith, Science and Reason: Theology on the Cutting Edge*, 2nd ed. (Chicago: Midwest Theological Forum, 2019).

8. See, e.g., Baglow, *Faith, Science, and Reason*.

9. Antony Flew, "Letter from Antony Flew on Darwinism and Theology," *Philosophy Now* 47 (August/September 2004), https://philosophynow.org/issues/47/Letter_from_Antony_Flew_on_Darwinism_and_Theology.

10. For more of MacIntyre's story, see Stanley Hauerwas, "The Virtues of Alasdair MacIntyre," *First Things*, October 2007, https://www.firstthings.com/article/2007/10/the-virtues-of-alasdair-macintyre.

11. Stanley Fish, *Winning Arguments: What Works and Doesn't Work in Politics, the Bedroom, the Courtroom, and the Classroom* (New York: HarperCollins, 2016), 29. The story about the agenda of doubt is based on the painstakingly

researched book by Naomi Oreskes and Erik Conway, *Merchants of Doubt: How a Handful of Scientists Obscured the Truth on Issues from Tobacco Smoke to Global Warming* (London: Bloomsbury, 2010).

12. See, e.g., the great work of the Center for Literacy Education at the University of Notre Dame, under the leadership of Ernest Morrell: https://iei .nd.edu/initiatives/cle.

13. Raymond Nickersen, "Confirmation Bias: A Ubiquitous Phenomenon in Many Guises," *Review of General Psychology* 2 (1998): 175–220; Barbara Koslowski, "Scientific Reasoning: Explanation, Confirmation Bias, and Scientific Practice," in *Handbook of the Psychology of Science*, ed. G. J. Feist and M. E. Gorman (New York: Springer, 2013), 151–92; Nardi, *Critical Thinking*, 110.

14. On biased reason, see Dan Sperber and Hugo Mercier, *The Enigma of Reason* (Princeton: Princeton University Press, 2019), 205–21.

Chapter 7: Without Order There Is No Good Reasoning

1. For a more detailed discussion, see Peter Coffey, *The Science of Logic: An Inquiry into the Principles of Accurate Thought and Scientific Method* (London: Longmans, Green, 1912), 2:10–22.

2. There are different understandings of coherence, but mine is shaped by Richard Swinburne, *The Coherence of Theism* (Oxford: Clarendon, 1993), 11–50.

Chapter 8: Ignorance Is Not Bliss

1. For a more detailed discussion, see Steve Vanderheiden, "The Obligation to Know: Information and the Burdens of Citizenship," *Ethical Theory and Moral Practice* 19 (2016): 297–311; Michael J. Zimmerman, *Ignorance and Moral Obligation* (Oxford: Oxford University Press, 2014); Daniel DeNicola, *Understanding Ignorance: The Surprising Impact of What We Don't Know* (Boston: MIT Press, 2017), 97–114; Miranda Fricker, *Epistemic Injustice: Power and the Ethics of Knowing* (Oxford: Oxford University Press, 2007). Although I disagree with the approach and conclusions in Dan Sperber and Hugo Mercier, *The Enigma of Reason* (Princeton: Princeton University Press, 2019), 110–27, I learned a lot from them regarding reasons as social constructs and how people can be mistaken about the reasons for their actions.

2. Lee Sigelman, "Is Ignorance Bliss? A Reconsideration of the Folk Wisdom," *Human Relations* 34, no. 11 (November 1981): 965–74.

3. Matthew J. Sheridan and Timothy E. Steele-Dadzie, "Structure of Intellect and Learning Style of Incarcerated Youth Assessment," *Journal of Correctional Education* 56 (2005): 347–71. A helpful and popular handbook regarding personal discipline is Harris Kern and Adriana Ace Castle, *Discipline: Take Control of Your Life* (Bloomington, IN: Authorhouse, 2011).

4. See Camilla Groth, Maarit Mäkelä, and Pirita Seitamaa-Hakkarainen, "Tactile Augmentation: A Multimethod for Capturing Experiential Knowledge," *Craft Research* 6 (2015): 57–81. In my book *God Is Not Nice* (Notre Dame, IN: Ave Maria, 2017), I have further developed an approach for seeing things hidden

in everyday life, but I also recommend the classic E. F. Schumacher, *Small Is Beautiful: Economics as if People Mattered* (New York: Harper & Row, 1978). On the virtues and vices of ignorance see DeNicola, *Understanding Ignorance*, 115–33.

5. See Plato, *Apology* 21c–d; *Charmides* 165b, 166c. See also Gail Fine, "Does Socrates Claim to Know That He Knows Nothing?," *Oxford Studies in Ancient Philosophy* 35 (2008): 49–88, which explains the background of the saying and its philosophical significance.

6. See the fantastic books by Stuart Firestein, *Ignorance: How It Drives Science* (Oxford: Oxford University Press, 2012), and *Failure: Why Science Is So Successful* (Oxford: Oxford University Press, 2015).

7. DeNicola, *Understanding Ignorance*, 65–78. See also ibid., 31–45 on "dwelling in ignorance."

Chapter 9: Real Thinking Sets You Free

1. Thornton Wilder, *The Ides of March* (New York: Harper, 1948), 34.

2. Many Americans do not know about the brutality of the Communist regime in Eastern Germany. For a first orientation, see John O. Koehler, *Stasi: The Untold Story of the East German Secret Police* (Boulder, CO: Westview, 1999); and Jonathan Sperber, "17 June 1953: Revisiting a German Revolution," *German History* 22 (2004): 619–43.

3. Aloys Wenzl, *Philosophie der Freiheit* (Munich: Filser, 1947), 69 (author's translation).

4. Robert Spaemann, *Persons: The Difference between Someone and Something* (Oxford: Oxford University Press, 2017), 197–220; Harald Schöndorf, *Erkenntnistheorie* (Stuttgart: Kohlhammer, 2014), 70–81.

5. D. C. Schindler, *Freedom from Reality: The Diabolical Character of Modern Liberty* (Notre Dame, IN: University of Notre Dame Press, 2017), 279–362.

6. Schindler, *Freedom from Reality*, 209.

7. On the theory of forgiveness, see especially Klaus-Michael Kodalle, *Annäherungen an eine Theorie des Verzeihens* (Stuttgart: Steiner, 2006); and Kodalle, *Verzeihung denken: Die verkannte Grundlage humaner Verhältnisse* (Munich: Fink, 2013). I owe much to the beautiful chapter in Heidemarie Bennent-Vahle, *Mit Gefühl denken: Einblicke in die Philosophie der Emotionen* (Freiburg: Alber, 2013), 245–314.

8. Bennent-Vahle, *Mit Gefühl denken*, 252; see also Mariano Crespo, *Das Verzeihen: Eine philosophische Untersuchung* (Heidelberg: Winter, 2002), who follows the realist phenomenology of Dietrich von Hildebrand, *Ethics* (New York: Hildebrand, 2020); Adolf Reinach, "Concerning Phenomenology," trans. Dallas Willard, *The Personalist* 50, no. 2 (1969): 194–221; and Max Scheler, *Of the Eternal in Man*, trans. Bernard Noble (London: SCM, 1960).

Chapter 10: Thinking Happens in a Soul, Not a Computer

1. In this chapter I rely on Holm Tetens, *Gott denken: Ein Versuch über rationale Theologie* (Stuttgart: Reclam, 2015), 12–29.

2. Lynne Rudder Baker, "Third Person Understanding," in *The Nature and Limits of Human Understanding*, ed. Anthony Sandford (London: T&T Clark, 2003), 186–208.

3. Uwe Meixner, *Defending Husserl: A Plea in the Case of Wittgenstein & Company versus Phenomenology* (Berlin: de Gruyter, 2014), 174.

4. Michael Hauskeller, *Atmosphären erleben: Philosophische Untersuchungen zur Sinneswahrnehmung* (Berlin: Akademie-Verlag, 1995), 164. See also David Chalmers, *The Conscious Mind: In Search of a Fundamental Theory* (Oxford: Oxford University Press, 1996), 93–209.

5. Steven J. Jensen, *The Human Person: A Beginner's Thomistic Psychology* (Washington, DC: Catholic University of America Press, 2018). An exciting reading about this problem remains Paul Ricoeur, *Oneself as Another*, trans. Kathleen Blamey (Chicago: University of Chicago Press, 1992).

6. For the reader who wants more, see Edward Feser, *Philosophy of Mind* (Oxford: Oneworld, 2005).

7. Robert Epstein, "The Empty Brain," *Aeon*, May 2016, https://aeon.co/essays/your-brain-does-not-process-information-and-it-is-not-a-computer. For a good introduction to the problem of mind and soul, see Thomas M. Crisp, Steven L. Porter, and Gregg A. Ten Elshof, eds., *Neuroscience and the Soul: The Human Person in Philosophy, Science, and Theology* (Grand Rapids: Eerdmans, 2016); Stewart Goetz and Charles Taliaferro, *A Brief History of the Soul* (Oxford: Wiley-Blackwell, 2011).

8. The faulty logic can easily be seen if you remember that for a valid conclusion the subject and the predicate must be entailed in the first premise. Since the first premise states "All computers behave intelligently," you cannot bring "all beings" (including humans) into the conclusion. All you can arrive at as a conclusion is "All information processors behave intelligently."

9. Here I am indebted to the work of psychologist Robert Epstein; see www.drrobertepstein.com.

10. Godehard Brüntrup, "Überall Geist: Die Renaissance des Panpsychismus," *Herderkorrespondenz* 71 (2017): 44–47 (author's translation).

11. Godehard Brüntrup, "Emergent Panpsychism," in *Panpsychism: Contemporary Perspectives*, ed. Godehard Brüntrup and Ludwig Jaskolla (New York: Oxford University Press, 2016), 1–25.

12. For a Thomistic exposition of the intelligibility of the resurrection of the body, see Thomas J. White, *The Light of Christ: An Introduction to Catholicism* (Washington, DC: Catholic University of America Press, 2017), 279–87.

13. In this chapter, I rely to a great extent on Richard Swinburne, *The Evolution of the Soul* (Oxford: Oxford University Press, 1997); and Swinburne, *Are We Bodies or Souls?* (Oxford: Oxford University Press, 2019), but I am not following his dualism. See also Leo Scheffczyk, *Unsterblichkeit bei Thomas von Aquin auf dem Hintergrund der neueren Diskussion* (Munich: Verlag der Akademie der Wissenschaften, 1989); Raymond Hain, "Aquinas and Aristotelian Hylomorphism," in *Aristotle in Aquinas's Theology*, ed. Gilles Emery and Matthew Levering (Oxford: Oxford University Press, 2015), 48–69; Melissa Eitenmiller,

"On the Separated Soul according to St. Thomas Aquinas," *Nova et Vetera* 17 (2019): 57–91.

Chapter 11: Majority Rules Don't "Make" Truth

1. I am indebted here to the philosophy of meaning as put forth by Winfried Weier, *Gibt es objektive Wahrheit? Auseinandersetzung mit der neuzeitlichen Erkenntniskritik* (Paderborn: Schöningh, 2014).
2. The only study that treats this topic in detail is the massive book by Winfried Weier, *Sinn und Teilhabe: Das Grundthema der abendländischen Geistesentwicklung* (Munich: Pustet, 1970).
3. René Descartes, *Meditations on First Philosophy*, 2nd ed., ed. John Cottingham (Cambridge: Cambridge University Press, 2017). The contrast between Cartesian and scholastic doubt is presented by Etienne Gilson, *Thomist Realism and the Critique of Knowledge* (San Francisco: Ignatius, 2012), chap. 2.
4. See Josef Van Elten, "Fringsen: Hintergrund und Wirkung einer Predigt des Kölner Erzbischof Frings," *Geschichte in Köln* 63 (2019): 195–216.
5. For a brilliant refutation of all claims that science can provide a foundation for morality, see James D. Hunter and Paul Nedelisky, *Science and the Good: The Tragic Quest for the Foundations of Morality* (New Haven: Yale University Press, 2018).

Chapter 12: Real Thinking Discovers Causes

1. See the excellent discussion of causality in Edward Feser, *Scholastic Metaphysics: A Contemporary Introduction* (Piscataway, NJ: Editiones Scholasticae, 2014), 105–45.
2. By focusing on things that came into existence, I exclude here the God-question (God is uncaused). I also exclude the thought experiment of an eternal, always-existing universe. Saint Thomas Aquinas thought God could have created such an eternal world. See Ralph McInerny, *Thomas Aquinas* (Notre Dame, IN: University of Notre Dame Press, 1982), chap. 2.
3. See the discussion of this thought in Alvin Plantinga, *Where the Conflict Really Lies: Science, Religion, and Naturalism* (Oxford: Oxford University Press, 2011), 249–51.
4. An excellent popular introduction to this topic is William Lane Craig, *The Existence of God and the Beginning of the Universe* (San Bernardino, CA: Here's Life, 1979). Equally recommended is Edward Feser's *Five Proofs for the Existence of God* (San Francisco: Ignatius, 2017).
5. G. E. M. Anscombe, "'Whatever Has a Beginning of Existence Must Have a Cause': Hume's Argument Exposed," *Analysis* 34 (1974): 145–51; Feser, *Scholastic Metaphysics*, 112–14.
6. Joseph Geyser, *Allgemeine Philosophie des Seins und der Natur* (Paderborn: Schöningh, 1915), 108–16.
7. Stephen T. Davis, *Rational Faith: A Philosopher's Defense of Christianity* (Downers Grove, IL: InterVarsity, 2016), 29–46.

8. Remember that God is not "part" of the world! See, for example, Rudi te Velde, *Aquinas on God* (Aldershot: Ashgate, 2006), 123–46, or David Bentley Hart, *Atheist Delusions* (New Haven: Yale University Press, 2009).

Chapter 13: Thinking about Goods, Values, and Morality

1. Dan Sperber and Hugo Mercier, *The Enigma of Reason* (Princeton: Princeton University Press, 2019), 127.

2. Max Scheler, *Formalism in Ethics and Non-Formal Ethics of Values: A New Attempt toward the Foundation of an Ethical Personalism*, 5th rev. ed., trans. Manfred S. Frings and Roger L. Funk (Evanston, IL: Northwestern University Press, 1973).

3. See especially Dietrich von Hildebrand, *Ethics* (New York: Hildebrand, 2020), 48–50; Martin Cajthaml and Vlastimil Vohánka, *The Moral Philosophy of Dietrich von Hildebrand* (Washington, DC: Catholic University of America Press, 2019), 123–52.

4. Dietrich von Hildebrand, *What Is Philosophy?* (Milwaukee: Bruce, 1960); Hildebrand, *The Nature of Love* (South Bend, IN: St. Augustine's Press, 2009).

5. John Finnis, *Natural Law and Natural Rights* (Oxford: Clarendon, 1980); Jean Porter, *Nature as Reason: A Thomistic Theory of the Natural Law* (Grand Rapids: Eerdmans, 2004); Alasdair MacIntyre, *After Virtue*, 3rd ed. (Notre Dame, IN: University of Notre Dame Press, 2007).

Chapter 14: Thinking Saves Lives

1. I have learned much from the excellent essays in Gordon Moskowitz and Heidi Grant, eds., *The Psychology of Goals* (New York: Guilford, 2009). For self-control, see O. Stavrova, T. Pronk, and M. D. Kokkoris, "Choosing Goals That Express the True Self: A Novel Mechanism of the Effect of Self-Control on Goal Attainment," *European Journal of Social Psychology* 49 (2018): 1329–36, https://doi.org/10.1002/ejsp.2559.

2. Ignatius's *Spiritual Exercises* is a how-to book, which is why the text seems dry and inaccessible if not approached in the context and under the guidance of a retreat master. A good introduction is Raymond Gawronski, *A Closer Walk with Christ: A Personal Ignatian Retreat* (Detroit: Our Sunday Visitor, 2003).

3. See A. Kretschmer-Trendowicz, K. M. Schnitzspahn, L. Reuter, and M. Altgassen, "Episodic Future Thinking Improving Children's Prospective Memory Performance in a Complex Task Setting with Real Life Task Demands," *Psychological Research* 83, no. 3 (April 2019): 514–25; Gabriele Oettingen, A. Timur Sevincer, and Peter M. Gollwitzer, eds., *The Psychology of Thinking about the Future* (New York: Guilford, 2018); Franco Imoda, *The Spiritual Exercises and Psychology* (Rome: Editrice Pontificia Università Gregoriana, 1996).

4. Raymond DiGiuseppe, "The Nature of Irrational and Rational Beliefs: Progress in Rational Emotive Behavior Therapy," *Journal of Rational-Emotive and Cognitive-Behavior Therapy* 14 (1996): 5–28; Philip Hyland, Mark Shevlin, Gary Adamson, Daniel Boduszek, "The Organization of Irrational Beliefs in Posttraumatic

Stress Symptomology: Testing the Predictions of REBT Theory Using Structural Equation Modelling," *Journal of Clinical Psychology* 70 (2014): 48–59.

5. For a popular overview, see Albert Ellis, *The Myth of Self-Confidence: How Rational Emotive Behavior Therapy Can Change Your Life Forever* (New York: Prometheus, 2005). For a more scholarly description, see Albert Ellis and Debbie Ellis, *Rational Emotive Behavior Therapy: Theories of Psychotherapy* (Washington, DC: American Psychological Association, 2011).

6. Adapted from Albert Ellis, *How to Control Your Anxiety Before It Controls You* (New York: Citadel, 1998), 50–51.

Chapter 15: Empathy Is Achieved by Hard Thinking

1. For a guide to this school of thinking see Robert Sokolowski, *Introduction to Phenomenology* (Cambridge: Cambridge University Press, 1999).

2. Edith Stein, *Zum Problem der Einfühlung*, vol. 5 of *Gesammelte Werke* (Freiburg: Herder, 2008).

3. Edith Stein, *The Collected Works of Edith Stein*, 3rd ed., vol. 3, *On the Problem of Empathy* (Washington, DC: ICS, 1986).

4. Nicole Wolf, "Wie werde ich mensch? Annäherung an Edith Steins Beitrag zu einem christlichen Existenzdenken" (PhD thesis, University of Hildesheim, 2011), 55–56.

5. For biographical details, see Teresia R. Posselt, *Edith Stein: The Life of a Philosopher and Carmelite* (Washington, DC: ICS Publications, 2005). One of the best books on Stein is Alasdair MacIntyre, *Edith Stein—A Philosophical Prologue, 1913–1922* (New York: Sheed & Ward, 2006).

Chapter 16: Leadership, Values, and Your Thoughts

1. I profited much from Ole Fogh, *The Virtue of Leadership* (Copenhagen: Copenhagen Business School Press, 2008), 1–20. The best biography of Wallenstein is still the masterpiece by Golo Mann, *Wallenstein: His Life Narrated* (New York: Holt, Rinehart and Winston, 1976).

2. Lisa B. Ncybe, "Ubuntu: A Transformative Leadership Philosophy," *Journal of Leadership Studies* 4 (2010): 77–82.

3. See especially Augustine's *Against the Academicians* and *Confessions*. A good introduction to his thinking is provided by Etienne Gilson, *The Christian Philosophy of St. Augustine* (Providence: Cluny Media, 2020).

4. I owe this point to Jonathan K. Jefferson, Ira H. Martin, and Jake Owens, "Leader Development through Reading and Reflection," *Journal of Leadership Studies* 8 (2014): 67–75.

5. Tom Morris, *If Aristotle Ran General Motors: The New Soul of Business* (New York: Holt, 1997), 27.

6. *The Rule of St. Benedict in English*, trans. Timothy Fry (Collegeville, MN: Liturgical Press, 1981). A beautiful and accessible introduction to the wisdom of St. Benedict is J. Augustine Wetta, *Humility Rules: Saint Benedict's Twelve-Step Guide to Genuine Self-Esteem* (San Francisco: Ignatius, 2018).

7. E.g., Robert R. Williams, *Hegel's Ethics of Recognition* (Berkeley: University of California Press, 1998).

8. By far the best introduction to the virtues is Josef Pieper, *The Four Cardinal Virtues*, trans. Richard Winston, Clara Winston, Lawrence E. Lynch, and Daniel F. Coogan (Notre Dame, IN: University of Notre Dame Press, 1966).

Chapter 17: Creative Thinking Is Not a Mystery

1. Arthur Schopenhauer, *Sämtliche Werke*, vol. 2 (Munich: Piper, 1911), 446.

2. Charles Whiting, *Creative Thinking* (New York: Reinhold, 1958), 3, however, understands only useful new ideas as creative.

3. David Cahan, ed., *Hermann von Helmholtz and the Foundations of Nineteenth-Century Science* (Berkeley: University of California Press, 1994), 245–46.

4. J. S. Munk, "Christian Wolff on Ars Inveniendi and Perfection" (master's thesis, University of Utrecht, 2019); Manfred Kienpointner, "On the Art of Finding Arguments: What Ancient and Modern Masters of Invention Have to Tell Us about the 'Ars Inveniendi,'" *Argumentation* 11 (1997): 225–36; Theodore Kisiel, "Ars Inveniendi: A Classical Source for Contemporary Philosophy of Science," *Revue Internationale de Philosophie* 34 (1980): 130–54.

5. John E. Arnold, "Education for Innovation," in *A Source Book for Creative Thinking*, ed. S. J. Parnes and H. F. Harding (New York: Scribner's Sons, 1962), 127–38.

6. Thomas Vogel, *Breakthrough Thinking: A Guide to Creative Thinking and Idea Generation* (Cincinnati: HOW Books, 2014), 16ff.; Anna N. N. Hui, Mavis W. J. He, and Wan-Chi Wong, "Understanding the Development of Creativity across the Life Span," in *The Cambridge Handbook of Creativity*, ed. James C. Kaufmann and Robert J. Sternberg, 2nd ed., (Cambridge: Cambridge University Press, 2019), 69–87; and Robert Sternberg, "Enhancing People's Creativity," in Kaufmann and Sternberg, *Cambridge Handbook of Creativity*, 88–103.

7. See Aristotle, *Topica* 1.

8. "Door," *Cambridge Dictionary*, https://dictionary.cambridge.org/diction ary/english/door.

9. Vogel, *Breakthrough Thinking*, 14–22.

Chapter 18: Reasoning Helps Us Find Unity in a Divided World

1. For an overview, see Ursula Goldenbaum, "Leibniz, Wolff and Early Modern Theology," in *Oxford Handbook of Early Modern Theology, 1600–1800*, ed. Ulrich L. Lehner, Richard A. Muller, and A. G. Roeber (Oxford: Oxford University Press, 2016), 550–63.

2. An excellent collection of essays on personhood is J. Wentzel van Huyssteen and Erik P. Wiebe, eds., *In Search of Self: Interdisciplinary Perspectives on Personhood* (Grand Rapids: Eerdmans, 2011); on connectedness in a business context, see Tom Morris, *If Aristotle Ran General Motors: The New Soul of Business* (New York: Holt, 1997), 179–82; on connectedness in the context of health care, see Rudolf C. K. P. Martinez, "Lost Touch: Situating Human-Connectedness in

Technology Caring in the Health Sciences," *Journal of Medical Investigation* 66 (2019): 12–14, and Sharon L. Latimer, "Human Connectedness in Nursing: A Case Study," *Contemporary Nurse* 44 (2013): 45–46; on connectedness in nature and its implications, I found helpful Joanne Vining, Melinda Merrick, and Emily Price, "The Distinction between Humans and Nature: Human Perceptions of Connectedness to Nature and Elements of the Natural and Unnatural," *Human Ecology Review* 15 (2008): 1–11.

3. For the importance of spiritual well-being and having a spiritual home, see Morris, *If Aristotle Ran General Motors.*

4. This insight is far too little appreciated. See Helmuth Plessner, *The Limits of Community: A Critique of Social Radicalism*, trans. Andrew Wallace (New York: Humanities Press, 1999).

5. On "home" as a place of belonging, see Paul O'Connor, *Home: The Foundations of Belonging* (London: Taylor & Francis, 2017), and especially Maria Montserrat, *Belonging: Solidarity and Division in Modern Societies* (Cambridge: Cambridge University Press, 2013).

6. "Truth Seeking, Democracy, Freedom of Thought and Expression—A Statement by Robert P. George and Cornel West," James Madison Program, March 18, 2017, https://jmp.princeton.edu/statement.

Index

Made in the USA
Monee, IL
27 August 2022

12699362R00114